UNCOMMON STORIES FROM EVERYDAY NAZARENES

ARCHITECTS
of the
ENDURING

UNCOMMON STORIES
FROM EVERYDAY
NAZARENES

Compiled and Edited
by
NEIL B. WISEMAN
and
L. WAYNE SEARS

Beacon Hill Press of Kansas City
Kansas City, Missouri

Copyright 2001
by Beacon Hill Press of Kansas City

Printed in the
United States of America

ISBN 083-411-8971

Cover Design: Paul Franitza

Library of Congress Cataloging-in-Publication Data

Uncommon stories from everyday Nazarenes / compiled and edited by Neil B. Wiseman and L. Wayne Sears.
   p. cm. — (Architects of the enduring)
  ISBN 0-8341-1897-1 (pbk.)
   1. Church of the Nazarene—History. I. Wiseman, Neil B. II. Sears, L. Wayne, 1917- III. Series.

BX8699.N33 U63 2001
287.9'9'09—dc21

                                     2001025889

10   9   8   7   6   5   4   3   2   1

Contents

Introduction

Architects use creativity and skills to forge many different materials and textures into stately libraries, gigantic malls, grand hotels, impressive banks, and magnificent homes. But eventually even their most substantial structures fall into ruin, and passersby wonder who the people who lived in the building were and what their story was.

The apostle Paul had in mind a much more enduring building when he wrote under the leadership of the Holy Spirit: "God is building a home. He's using us all—irrespective of how we got here—in what he is building. He used the apostles and prophets for the foundation. Now he's using you, fitting you in brick by brick, stone by stone, with Christ Jesus as the cornerstone" (Eph. 2:19-20, TM).

This book is about that much more enduring building Paul described so well. It's about architects and builders who partnered with the Master Craftsman to build eternal materials like redemption, restoration, and reconciliation into the people of God—His Church.

In a sermon preached sometime before 1903, Phineas F. Bresee, founder of the Church of the Nazarene in the West and perhaps its most visible architect, beautifully described the dedication, sacrifice, and focus he considered necessary for early Nazarenes to possess: "When Garibaldi was raising his army, he said, 'I have no money, no food, no clothing, no stores, no resources. Let every man who is willing to suffer poverty, shame, hunger, disease, death follow me.' God has called us to this work—to sacrifice and to toil, to devotion and hardship; to prayer and supplication, to proclamation and testimony. He has called us to a movement from which nothing can deviate us."

We honor these dauntless souls and others like them who experienced the indescribable ecstasy of doing enduring work for God.

A Holiness Oratorio

Before a concert, orchestra members must go through the process of tuning their instruments. From one basic tone, every player must bring his or her instrument into harmony with all the others. Each will play a series of different notes at different times and at various tempos. Sometimes during the preparation, one hears discordant, even rasping, noises and wonders how anything tuneful and inspiring could be produced from such incoherent sound.

Then, when the conductor is satisfied and raises his or her arms to begin, he or she looks at all the assembled musicians to get their undivided attention. When the conductor's arms sweep down and the orchestra responds, one is carried away on a flood of music. Thrilling, inspiring, and deeply satisfying are the sounds. Harmony and pure music flow from a group of divergent people under the leadership of a master musician.

The Church of the Nazarene has formed such a group. This book singles out some of the players, representative of myriads of others who, under the baton of the Holy Spirit, produced a great oratorio. Many had little formal training, their instruments were sometimes crude makeshifts, and they were as varied in background as any group ever assembled. But their union produced a community of holy joy. With the starry heavens for a sound chamber, the empty plains, squalid cities, and small towns for a stage, they echoed the music of heaven, whose eternal theme is "Holiness unto the Lord."

Only God can imagine what this new century will produce if our Lord tarries. But even now, with 135 world areas adding their own distinctive themes to the chorus, we eagerly anticipate the time when "the whole world give[s] back the song / Which now the angels sing."

The score for this oratorio is the Holy Bible, the Word of God. "For prophecy never had its origin in the will of man, but men spoke from God as they were carried along by the Holy Spirit" (2 Pet. 1:21). The author, then, is God himself, "For this is what the high and lofty One says—he who lives forever, whose name is holy: 'I live in a high and holy place, but also with him who is contrite and lowly in spirit'" (Isa. 57:15). The musicians must not alter or change the score, but play it as the Author intended. They are responsible only to understand it as best as they can and play under the direction of the Holy Spirit, who is the Conductor and knows what each instrument can and should produce. The musicians are made worthy to play in this orchestra by "the blood of Christ, who through the eternal Spirit offered himself unblemished to God, [cleansing] our consciences from acts that lead to death, so that we may serve the living God!" (Heb. 9:14).

There is a "lost chord" in the music of the world—the loss of holiness and the image of God. Disobedience entered and brought the disharmony of sin. When all the evils of sin are banished forever from the universe, God's great orchestra will sound the triumphant grand Amen.

The Hallelujah March following the motion for union of the North and the South at Pilot Point, 1908.

I—A Charge to Keep I Have

The Yankee Who Sacrificed His Gold Watch for Unity: William Howard Hoople

William Howard Hoople was the son of a millionaire leather merchant in New York City. Much of his fortune was likely made supplying the Union Army during the Civil War. The merger meeting of various groups that formed the Church of the Nazarene at Pilot Point, Texas, included many impoverished former Southerners, such as C. B. Jernigan.

The story of the early beginnings of the Church of the Nazarene revolves around the differences between these two men, and those like them. Hoople and Jernigan represented many of the differences, both sectional and cultural, that had to be surmounted before a truly national church could be formed.

Hoople was converted in a Dwight L. Moody revival in Brooklyn, New York, in January 1886. In the early 1890s he began attending a noonday prayer meeting at the John Street Methodist Episcopal Church. There he met with Charles Bevier, who was a strong witness to holiness. Bevier was the choir leader of the largest Methodist church in Brooklyn. Hoople was drawn to Bevier's experience with God but thought he was a bit too "fanatical." The friendship developed, but as Hoople sought to argue Bevier into a more reasonable attitude, he lost the argument and sought the blessing of heart holiness.

Soon afterward, Hoople and Bevier organized the Utica Avenue Tabernacle with a view to promoting holiness and serving the needs of the poor of that area. They also sponsored the emerging Pentecostal Alliance, an association of "second-blessing holiness" churches in New England.

Before the meeting of Holiness people from the East and the West at Chicago in 1907, Hoople was hesitant to unite with Bresee's group in California. Living in the glow and blessing of the experience of holiness, he feared any organization might quench the flame of personal experience. He also feared any kind of ecclesiasticism. But when Hoople and Bevier went West, they found the Nazarenes to be their own crowd. The waves of glad joy they experienced in the West convinced them that union was the proper action to take.

The day Hoople was sanctified, he felt called to preach and served the rest of his life as a bivocational pastor, evangelist, church planter, Northeastern home mission secretary and field superintendent, New York district superintendent in 1908, and chaplain to United States troops in World War I in France, Italy, and Siberia. He refused salaries, funding his ministry from his business enterprises.

When the meeting in Pilot Point convened in 1908, William Howard Hoople was a representative from the Alliance. In his dress he was a sharp contrast to the poorer, more plainly clad representatives, particularly those from the Southwest who included Southerners who had moved West after the Civil War.

Those who met at Pilot Point were inescapably a part of the national picture of the divisions that resulted from that tragic war. That period had seen the nation ruptured, families divided, parents separated from their children. It had also seen the split of older denominations so that they did not begin to renew their historic ties for 50 years or so.

As the movement toward unity progressed at Pilot Point, there was little difficulty with doctrine. They knew the biblical holiness passages well, and John Wesley was frequently quoted.

But when they began to write the rules for conduct, the regional differences, prejudices, habits, and culture began to arise. The Southwesterners particularly had strong convictions on many points. They believed their convictions were God-given; thus, there was little room for compromise.

As the debates concerning the rules continued, Phineas F. Bresee from California, the chairman of the meeting, paced back and forth across the platform, holding his head in his hands. He begged the delegates not to "bring the doctrine of holiness of heart down to the level of a set of rules."

Worldly adornment was a critical issue. With his expensive gold watch and chain across his expansive waist, Hoople was very noticeable. When it looked as though they had reached an impasse and all hope for a national church seemed gone, an electrifying thing happened.

William Howard Hoople arose from his seat, strode to the edge of the tent, drew his gold watch and chain from his vest, and announced, "If eating meat offends my brother, I will eat no meat while the world stands!" Then he hurled the watch and chain as far as he could into the prairie grass that surrounded the tent.

That gesture by that sanctified man encouraged the unity that finally prevailed.

—*Raymond W. Hurn*

Good Religion Makes a Rebel
Hug a Yankee: C. B. Jernigan

In 1863 at the Jernigan plantation near Vicksburg, Mississippi, a Black slave woman rushed to Mrs. C. B. Jernigan, screaming that a troop of Yankee soldiers was coming. Mrs. Jernigan hurried to the gate and confronted the captain.

"What do you want?" she challenged.

"We are going to take what we want and burn the rest," the captain replied.

Mrs. Jernigan pulled a large revolver from under her skirts and replied, "Over my dead body!" The captain hesitated a moment, then ordered his men to ride on.

Three months later, a son was born to Mrs. Jernigan. She named him Charles Brougher Jernigan. Her husband, a doctor and a captain in the Confederate army, returned after the war. The ravages of the war and the "carpetbaggers" following the war years brought the family to the level of destitution. They loaded what they had left of worldly goods in a prairie schooner and moved to Texas.

C. B. Jernigan grew up in Texas and matured into an enterprising, brave, and tenacious man who refused to admit defeat. Perhaps that is best illustrated by an event that happened after he was district superintendent of an area that covered Texas, Oklahoma, and Kansas. He received a letter from a prospective pastor from another denomination asking what he had to offer. Jernigan replied that the kind of men who would succeed in Oklahoma were men who would "take the bull by the horns, break his neck, skin him and make a tent of his hide, and peddle the meat for a living. I know the pasture that the bull runs in, and if you will come over, I will show him to you. Come on."

During his lifetime as evangelist, pastor, and district superintendent, C. B. Jernigan organized 130 new churches, founded the town of Bethany, Oklahoma, and built a stone auditorium there that some called "Jernigan's folly." The building would seat nearly 300 people, and most members of the church said there would never be a Nazarene congregation that large.

At the Pilot Point Assembly in 1908, his voice was heard and respected. The East and the West that had come together in Chicago in 1907 were eager for him and the others from the Southwest to join.

Rev. Jernigan was also eager to unite with the emerging denomination but not at the price of compromise in any of their positions. Therefore, he was a strong exponent of strict rules of conduct. Then he saw Hoople throw away his gold watch. That Yankee! That rich man with money that represented the loss of his father's plantation!

The doctrine of perfect love he espoused became operationally relevant to the situation. In Hoople he saw another man as devoted as he was to the doctrine of perfect love, and by his renewed nature he called him "Brother." When the assembly was ready to vote, he rose and made another electrifying statement: "I have never hugged a Yankee before, but I am going to hug one now!" And he proceeded to hug Hoople as a long-lost brother.

—*L. Wayne Sears*

The Little Giant Who Loved
Sunday Comics and Radio: E. P. Ellyson

A short, quiet, little, cherub-faced man disturbed the saints at Michigan's Indian Lake Nazarene Campgrounds with a radio and a newspaper. He was reading the comics and turning up the volume on his radio on Sundays. He liked the Sunday comics, and he had to have the radio loud to counteract his growing deafness. The radio was a new invention and, therefore, suspect. No self-respecting Holiness believer would read the comics on God's holy day, because comics kept the reader from spiritual thoughts and gave the devil's crowd something to do to keep them busy on the day they should be in church.

The problem was greatly compounded by the fact that this little man was a former general superintendent, former editor in chief of the Sunday School periodicals, former college professor, and former college president. Since there was little they could do, they sputtered while he read and enjoyed the radio.

Edgar P. Ellyson was elected at the Pilot Point Assembly as one of the first three general superintendents. At that historic meeting he represented the South; Bresee was from the West, H. F. Reynolds from the East. Ellyson served several colleges as president, including Peniel, Texas; and Pasadena, California.

E. P. Ellyson was an effective evangelist and a fervent preacher of the doctrine of holiness as a second definite work of grace. His association with Phineas F. Bresee dated back to Los Angeles First Church when Bresee was the pastor. As a general superintendent, Ellyson worked with his colleagues to establish the denomination and its doctrinal position. The task was not without its difficulties. The salary was small, so he depended on his salary as president of Texas Holiness University for his home expenses. Education was such a high priority for him that when reelected to the office of general superintendent, he declined, choosing rather to continue his ministry in education.

In his retirement years, it was natural for him to return to his cottage at Indian Lake, Michigan. Here he could enter into the many camp activities and visit often with old friends. His daughter lived there, and with her care, he could live a leisurely life. It was there on a Sunday afternoon that I first saw him. I was a new, young Christian ready to accept anything the church expected of me. But my grandmother was very disturbed about the Sunday comics and the blaring popular music.

This incident serves as an example of the unity and diversity of early Nazarene leaders. They believed in unity, but not uniformity. Some have pictured the early Nazarenes as tight-lipped, stern fundamentalists marching lockstep with no deviations, wearing their "holiest frowns." Such was far from the truth.

—*E. Drell Allen*

Thank God for Speech Teachers: Louise Dygoski

Every local Church of the Nazarene owes much to the speech instructors who worked so hard to teach preachers how to speak effectively. That is the difficult assignment Louise Dygoski performed so well for many years at Eastern Nazarene College. In her journey of faithful service, she moved from bookkeeper to speech instructor and made a tremendous contribution to the ministry of many future pastors.

The Great Depression years were exceedingly difficult for teaching faculties in Nazarene colleges. Professors were promised small salaries, and often the colleges could not fulfill their promises. Those who kept the books experienced even greater levels of stress. So often they wrestled the challenge of how to pay the necessary bills while keeping some money for token payments to the faculty.

Louise Dygoski, bookkeeper at Eastern Nazarene College in the late 1930s, is a prime example of a dedicated person charged with such crushing responsibilities. On a cold day in November, Louise closed the thick financial journal and prayed for help. Faculty families often had to get food from the college kitchen when they had no money. The struggle for survival kept morale at a low ebb. Where could one turn? *O God,* she prayed, *You have promised that if we call upon You, You would deliver us. Now is a good time to answer.*

And answer He did.

Louise was a petite young woman, meticulous in everything she did and said. She had strength and dignity, was humble and unassuming, and possessed a great sense of humor.

The college survived the depression, and when G. B. Williamson assumed the presidency, he led them into a state of solvency. But Dr. Williamson did more than solve the financial problems. Among many other impressive accomplishments, he encouraged Louise to pursue her interest in public speaking by earning an advanced degree. She was a superior student of speech with Mrs. Williamson and of literature with Dean Munro. As a result, when Dr. Williamson moved to the pastorate of Kansas City First Church, Louise was chosen to fill Mrs. Williamson's position as instructor in speech communication.

In 1960 Louise became the first woman of ENC's faculty to earn a Ph.D. She did this while teaching and studying at the University of Wisconsin. After that, she returned to her position and served there until her retirement. Across the years, other colleges and universities extended invitations with offers of salary increases, but her devotion to the mission of ENC kept her faithful to the task.

One of her many students wrote of Dr. Dygoski, "When I enrolled at ENC, I was told that I would have to take private speech lessons from Dr. Dygoski. I went to the lessons with fear and trepidation. But I found a lady who diagnosed the problem, and in one semester of private lessons the impediment was gone and I could communicate all sounds clearly and with confidence."

Like so many other dedicated teachers in Nazarene colleges, Louise had a vision of a mighty task—a life that, being lived, builds itself in the lives of others. Her pastor said of her, "Most of all, Louise Dygoski was a friend and servant of the Lord Jesus Christ. She loved words, but most of all she loved the Word. She knew the Word. She memorized the Word. She lived the Word. She never stood over the Word, but humbly sought to let it speak to her and in her and through her."

Her treasures are stored up in heaven and continue here on earth through the influence of her life on her students.

—*Marion K. Rich*

The Intercessor Who Impacted Many Lives: Naomi Cunningham

Naomi Cunningham was a prayer warrior of the old school, the kind who prayed and then went to work to help answer her own prayers.

Once a friend urged her postal carrier to ask Naomi about salvation. Naomi didn't just talk to him—she led him to the Lord. He later became the pastor of a large Baptist church on the south side of Chicago. She also used her telephone extensively for prayer, counseling, and encouragement.

In a message honoring pastors at the 1997 General Assembly in San Antonio, her son, General Superintendent Paul Cunningham, told of her dynamic strength of character: "I grew up going to church at 7:30 on Sunday nights in old Chicago First Church. When we changed our hour at College Church [in Olathe, Kansas] many years ago to 6:00, my mother thought I'd lost out spiritually. 'You're just compromising; you're just giving in, Paul; why don't you take a stand? Have church when God means for you to have church on Sunday nights.' Oh, I'd hate to ever have to tell my 91-year-old mother I was not having church on Sunday night! I'd be a dead man; I tell you that right now. I wouldn't mind facing the Board of General Superintendents—that'd be easy. But to face Naomi Pearl—that's another story."

Mrs. Martha Garvin, who sings and plays old songs on radio and televsion in the Chicago area on a program called "Musical Memories," spent an entire program telling about her "Aunt Naomi." Naomi and her husband, Paul, began singing soon after they were married. The songs were all of heartfelt, personal experience and praise, such as "It's Real," "A Child of the King," and "A Sinner like Me."

Mrs. Cunningham was 93 years of age when she went to be with her Lord. Because of declining health, she spent her last years in an extended care facility. Even there she found a ministry of encouragement. A new convert at Chicago First Church, Dave Blomgren, was asked to take some flowers and visit her. He thought he was to assure her of the continuing care of the church, but the pastor, Rev. Charles Higgins, had another purpose. He knew Dave needed her encouragement.

Listen to Dave's testimony of the visit. "The pastor asked me to deliver some flowers and other remembrances to a lady in a nursing home. He gave me the name of the nursing home and the location. He said the lady's name was Naomi Cunningham. Her name meant nothing to me, since I was a new member of the Church of the Nazarene.

"I arrived at the nursing home and was directed to her room, and there I met Naomi. The room was a typical, plain, no-frills room—one roommate and a picture or two adorning the walls. Yet I was not prepared for what happened next. This lady, who was confined to a room and bed, was the most alive and shining person I had ever met. She radiated sweetness and contentment and a spirit I had never observed in anyone. This for her was a place of life and continual celebration of Jesus.

"When I left the room, a tear rolled down my cheek as I recalled the lesson this wonderful servant of God had taught me: 'For I have learned to be content in whatever circumstances I am. I know how to get along with humble means, and I also know how to live in prosperity; in any and every circumstance I have learned the secret of being filled and going hungry, both of having abundance and suffering need. I can do all things through Him who strengthens me' [Phil. 4:11-13, NASB]."

—*Joanne Cunningham Carlson*

Pastor Extraordinaire Elected to the Beer Board: H. H. Wise

The heavyset, sad-eyed man stood tall in any room. His cheeks were lined, his jaws sagging, his shoulders bent. Tucked under one arm was a large Bible, the pages dog-eared and worn. The pockets of his black suit were lumpy and bulging. All this made the new class secretly skeptical of his reputation as a great Bible teacher. After all, by trade he was a plasterer; he had constructed a church building with his own hands. He sensed the tension and told an anecdote that left the class shaking with laughter.

Henry Howard Wise was born in Stonefort, Illinois, on January 20, 1889. He moved to Nashville around 1908 to enter Rev. J. O. McClurkan's Literary and Bible Training School, the forerunner of Trevecca Nazarene University. While a student, he conducted home Bible studies in West Nashville. From these studies came the core of people who later became the congregation of McClurkan Memorial Church of the Nazarene. Theirs was the church building he constructed with his own hands and served there for nine years.

From West Nashville, Wise went to Trevecca as business manager and field representative. In 1921 he was elected superintendent of the Tennessee District and served for only one year while he continued working at the college. In his report to the district assembly he stated that he had accepted other work and was thus not eligible for reelection. This other work was the pastorate of Nashville First Church, which he assumed for the remainder of his life, 26 years.

There was no pomposity about H. H. Wise. He knew his people with an intimacy that came from serving them well, growing with them, dedicating their infants, marrying their young, and burying their dead. Before the word "empathy" was in vogue, H. H. Wise personified it by faithful visits to the hospitals and jail, the penitentiary and slum homes, the asylum and "old-folks' home." He witnessed a number of executions in the electric chair. He sent letters regularly to every person in the congregation who was serving in the military. He wrote monthly letters to each shut-in. Funeral directors learned that he would conduct a funeral regardless of church affiliation or its lack. For years he kept a scrapbook of funerals he conducted until he passed the 5,000 mark.

Because of his interest in the moral climate of his city, he sought and secured a position on the Nashville Beer Board, reasoning that if he could not stop liquor traffic, he could at least help control its distribution. He did not hesitate to call personally on judges for help in taking neglected children away from their parents "to give them a chance."

Trevecca Nazarene University survived during 1934-35 because H. H. Wise made the Nashville First Church facilities available for the school's use. For years he taught two courses at Trevecca—Bible and practical theology. Frequently, ministerial students became his interns, most complaining that they had never worked so hard. More than once First Church gave the equivalent of entire congregations to start other churches in the city. God blessed this effort, and the congregation increased from approximately 227 to nearly 1,000 during his years of service.

The church sanctuary grew so crowded on Sunday mornings that it became almost an obsession with Wise to build a new sanctuary. The first Sunday of each month was Building Fund Sunday, and he guarded this fund more zealously than if every cent were his own. He made do with a meager salary and paid his own utilities at the parsonage, while he watched that fund swell. When it reached $100,000, he promised, construction would begin. At his death, the congregation was astonished to learn that approximately $92,000 had been accumulated.

Pastor Wise had not been well for several years, and his doctor repeatedly warned him of the danger of overtaxing himself. There was so much to be done, and he so loved doing it that he could not find a place to stop. On August 21, 1948, not quite 60 years of age, Wise concluded work for the next day's sermon, titled "Christian Certitude and Assurance." The last paragraph closed with 1 Cor. 15:55-57: "O death, where is thy sting? O grave, where is thy victory? The sting of death is sin; and the strength of sin is the law. But thanks be to God, which giveth us the victory through our Lord Jesus Christ." Within less than two hours, Wise suffered a heart attack and died at his post of duty, where he had always wished to be when called to heaven. Attendance at his funeral was estimated at 5,000, a tribute to the love and esteem in which he was held.

According to many, H. H. Wise was easily the most well known and loved minister in the city of Nashville and probably did more than any other person to establish the solid reputation of the Nazarene denomination in Tennessee and surrounding states.

—William M. Greathouse

——— ✠ ———

Making the Great Commission Personal at the Mother Church: Paul W. Benefiel

God led a baby born in the basement of a small church in Alva, Oklahoma, to go as an adult pastor to the mother Nazarene congregation in Los Angeles to lead it to become a reenergized example of the denomination's early commitment to evangelize every culture in the world.

This person would become an outstanding instrument of God's Spirit to achieve unity in the racially mixed, culturally diverse environment of California. Paul W. Benefiel was the name given to this child. His father pastored the Alva church, and his family lived in the basement.

After the family settled in California, Paul proved to be a leader in high school. He entered Pasadena College, now Point Loma Nazarene University, with thoughts of becoming an attorney at law. The Lord had other plans, however, and directed him toward pastoral ministry. From the start, he felt God leading him to a ministry that would welcome all people in the great traditions of the church. So, along with his theological training, he earned a master's degree in sociology from the University of Southern California.

Over a span of years, he and his wife, Pearle, and their five children served California pastorates in Wilmington, Brea, Pomona, and Los Angeles First. In addition, through teaching sociology at Pasadena College, he expressed his passion for taking the gospel to all people, and he participated in many community efforts. This approach to the pastoral ministry brought the blessing of the Lord. The churches grew not only in numbers but also in love and care for persons of many nationalities and backgrounds.

It was fitting that the "mother church" of the West should be the scene of his most influential and last pastorate. While Benefiel was at Los Angeles First Church, the community around the church changed dramatically. Rather than move away to a "better location," the congregation chose to minister to the world at their doorstep. Their seizing this golden opportunity resulted in launching a Spanish-speaking congregation that has become one of the largest in the denomination. Other ethnic starts included Korean and Filipino churches.

Sensing the new ministry changes all around them, the Los Angeles District in 1975 elected Dr. Benefiel as their district superintendent. During the next 17 years the number of churches on the district grew from 76 to 98, with another 20 operating as mission-type churches. In that period the district received 15,269 members by profession of faith, ordained 104 as elders, and received an additional 16 ministers by recognition of elder's orders.

During that vastly changing time, a typical district missionary convention service would encompass people from all nationalities and walks of life. A Korean children's choir, a Black gospel choir, a Filipino soloist, and congregational singing in Spanish, Armenian, Chinese, as well as English would all be a part of the ministry. As diverse congregations sang in the unity of the Spirit "To God Be the Glory," it was difficult not to think of Pentecost. Thank God for the extension of the unity at Pilot Point, where the saintly Phineas F. Bresee, the first pastor of Los Angeles First Church, played so large a part in the uniting General Assembly of 1908.

—*Dick Willis*

Get the Chairs Ready for a Day of Miracle: Ambrozina Azevedo

When Ambrozina Azevedo accepted Christ, her life took unexpected turns. A widow and a teacher in Praia, the capital city of Cape Verde, she was immediately called to the principal's office and ordered to renounce her new faith. As a widow with a daughter, she desperately needed that job. But when she refused to renounce her newfound faith, the principal fired her on the spot.

Missionaries Everette and Garnet Howard were supportive of their new convert. The Praia congregation surrounded Doña Ambrozina. She started crocheting, baking, and cooking to support her daughter.

Doña Ambrozina was one of my childhood Sunday School teachers. Twenty years later, when she was in her 60s, I became her pastor. At the installation service, she assured me of her prayers and support, a priceless gift to a young minister in his first pastorate. My visits to her modest home would invariably end with a word of prayer. Then she would ask to pray for me—my favorite part of the visit.

But there was a day when I wished she had been quiet. It was the last Sunday of January in 1964. A letter from our headquarters in Kansas City challenged all Nazarene churches to a record attendance on Easter Sunday, March 29. I decided to take the issue to the congregation for a goal they would embrace, support, and reach. We were proud of our previous record of 317. What goal should we now have for Easter Sunday?

At that stage of my presentation, the question was rhetorical rather than an inquiry. But Doña Ambrozina stood up and shocked us all. "Pastor," she said, "we should go for 1,000!" It was not a joke. Doña Ambrozina's face was serious, her eyes misty. No one laughed; they respected her too much to do so. Then I did what most pastors do when they're not sure what to say. "Let us pray," I announced.

That prayer time became an electrifying experience in my ministry. Someone had taken hold of the congregation. The number "1,000" popped up from prayers coming from fired-up

Nazarenes. When the prayers subsided, I conceded, "We're going to have 1,000—it will be our day of miracle."

"Yes!" Doña Ambrozina said. "I like it—'our day of miracle'!" The phrase became our motto. For the next few weeks, it would be found on bumper stickers, posters, flyers, letters, notes, and in telephone calls.

"Pastor, you will need room and seats for 1,000," Doña Ambrozina reminded me on my next visit. "I have two or three extra chairs. You had better take them to the church and, like the widow from Scripture who borrowed vessels, find many, many more chairs." The following weeks were frantic for the whole congregation—installation of a new sound system with wiring to the youth auditorium, to Sunday School classes, and to the churchyard. And yes, chairs. Dozens of members and the pastor knocked on doors around the city inviting people and borrowing chairs for 'our day of miracle.'" It was the talk of the town. On Easter Sunday they came from everywhere. The 20 members trained to greet and count the worshipers presented the attendance count to the pastor: 1,863.

Doña Ambrozina was crying silently. Later she explained, "I saw the beginning of this work, when we were fired from our jobs, stoned, despised, and persecuted. We were then a handful. Now to see this crowd in our church listening reverently to the message of Christ—this is beyond all dreams." And then she whispered to me, "Pastor, please keep those chairs from my house; you will need them, because this church will never be the same again after our day of miracle." She was right.

Soon we organized a new church with an attached day school in the neighboring community of Achada de Santo Antonio, today one of the leading Nazarene churches of Cape Verde. Enthusiastic groups of young people conducted weekly services and had Sunday School in nine sites in the outskirts of the city.

Ambrozina Azevedo promised and challenged these young workers: "I'll be praying for you while you minister. Be bold. Go in the power of the Spirit."

The central church was growing. On Tuesday evenings, close to 200 youth crowded in for the young people's meeting. It was time to remodel—build a new youth auditorium, more Sunday

School classrooms, day school facilities, and a close-by fellowship hall. The church board agreed. Blueprints were submitted to the city authorities. Their answer was a bombshell. Not only was the permit denied, but a note attached to the document stated, "This building will be removed." We were told the decision was from the governor. The intolerant dictatorship then ruling the country was capable of bulldozing our building. Our Easter attendance that had brought to the Nazarene church over one-tenth of the city's population had infuriated the establishment.

Now we were facing a real emergency. Leaders of the congregation rushed to a meeting "to consider options and agree on strategies." The mood was somber. Phrases like "lawyers," "lawsuit," "cable Kansas City," and "contact the Ministry of Justice in Portugal" were being tossed from all directions. In the midst of all that confusion, Doña Ambrozina mumbled these words: "a strategy of prayer." She pulled us back to our true foundation. And pray we did. On my request, she led us. Calmly, as someone with high connections, Ambrozina Azevedo talked to God. After our "amens," she looked straight at me and said, "Pastor, this building is *not* going to be removed, but the governor who said so will be." I nodded respectfully with a faith quite a bit smaller than a "mustard seed."

Two days later the city was buzzing with news: "The governor has been transferred to another province." Ambrozina smiled quietly, as someone who knows a precious secret. A new ruler arrived, reversed the previous threat that had condemned our building, and ordered that we receive a remodeling permit "today, no questions asked." That very week we started extensive remodeling work. In August 1989 the church that had been condemned to be removed received one of the highest honors in any country: it was depicted on a postal stamp now valued by collectors all over the world.

In May 1980 my wife and I received a poem from Doña Ambrozina. On an attached note, she said that it was a good-bye message "because it is now time to go home." Days later, at age 92, she was finally at home with Christ, the Choice of her life.

—*Jorge M. S. Barros*

The Boilermaker Who Planted Churches: Frank Dean

Papa was saved at 17 under the ministry of Brother Tidwell in Chattanooga, Tennessee. When I moved to Nashville, he told me that if I were ever tempted to think I was "big stuff," I was only a two-hour drive from humility. "Just go over to the other side of the tracks in Chattanooga where your daddy was when the church found him for God."

Brother Tidwell was very strict about a lot of things. I asked Papa if he believed the way Brother Tidwell did about coffee and neckties and other "no-no's." He said, "I believed that those people loved me, and that felt a whole lot better than coffee ever tasted."

Papa loved the church and would often say to me, "The church owes us nothing. We owe the church everything." We served on the church board together for only one year. When I complained about another board member who was always "dragging his feet," he gave me one of his lessons: "A clock has to have a fast hand and a slow hand to tell time. You're our fast hand; he's the slow one."

Papa was a layman. He was a boilermaker and worked all over the eastern United States building power plants. Often when he would finish a job, he would take me with him to the union hall and "sign the book" to be sent on another project. The business manager, Mr. Curry, was always very friendly and respectful to Papa. I asked Papa if he was Mr. Curry's best friend. He told me that he didn't have to be Mr. Curry's best friend—he was his best welder. From him I learned that I should never let my livelihood depend on who I knew but only on how well I did my work.

Wherever he worked for several months, his goal was to plant a Nazarene church there. There would be a tent and services every night until there were enough converts to form a congregation. He loved to go back to those churches to see how they had grown. I recently heard someone extolling the virtues of the "staff-driven church." Apparently Papa missed that concept. He loved to quote Vance Havner: "It's the preacher's job to fill the pulpit. It's our job to fill the pews."

He would do just about anything to fill those pews. There were contests between the Reds and the Blues. He gave bicycles and trips to Marineland for prizes. But the real prize was when someone was saved.

On Saturday mornings he would take me with him to visit the homes near whatever church we were planting. "You take this side of the street, and I'll take that one. Smile. Give them this paper about the church. Tell them we'd love to have them." If I complained about the heat or the length of the street, he would just hug me and say, "Karen, we're God's spending money. He can use us however He wants." Papa would even roll down the car window at a red light and ask the people in the other lane if they had a church home.

I think the term we use today is "discipleship," but Papa was always "checking on people." When he was away from people he had led to the Lord, he would write letters of blessing and encouragement to them, often on paper place mats from the diners where he ate. "I was sitting here in Paducah, Kentucky, thinking about you and wanting you to know that I'm praying for you and counting on your prayers for me."

Children were a high priority for Papa and for any church where he was working. They flocked to him. He said he was taking good care of the folks who were going to push his wheelchair someday. He tried to tell each of them what he always told us: "God is going to bless the world through you." He believed in education and helped so many of us through school that he said he was suffering from "maltuition."

Papa was a friend of the underdog. When we rode the bus into town in Jacksonville, Florida, he took me to the back where usually only Black people sat. He showed me the "White" and "Colored" signs behind the department store water fountains and made certain I knew that Jesus wanted these signs to come down—and that He would let me help Him take them down.

When Papa retired, he walked and biked several miles a day all over Jacksonville. On his rounds he discovered that stores were throwing away large quantities of good food. He began retrieving that food and distributing it to the rescue mission and directly to needy people. He drove a faded blue Toyota truck held together by bumper stickers from every Democrat who had run for office the previous decade. One day I was bumping along the railroad tracks with him to take some food boxes to the people who lived there. As we parked in front of one of the shacks, a stooped old man shouted to his wife, "Church Man is bringing you some more fruit cocktail, Mattie!"

On the way home that day, I said, "Papa, I hope that when I help people, I'll always treat them with love and dignity the way you do." I'll always remember his response: "Oh, Honey, we need them a lot more than they need us. They're the only way we have to send our love to Jesus."

World missions was a great passion for my father. Every time he had saved almost enough money to buy a car, someone would tell him about a new field that needed to be opened, and he was back at the bus stop. When Papa and Mother were getting ready for a Work and Witness trip, he would take buckets to local motels for them to save their slightly used bars of soap. He would wet them, press them together, and lay them in the sun on the back steps. The soap suitcase would be filled to the brim when they left. One day he went to pick up soap at the Marriott hotel. While he was there, the house manager asked if he would like to have the used sheets and towels. Of course he wanted them, and when he drove up to the house with a truckload of linen, he grinned, winked, and said, "I've never seen a Mormon [the Marriott family is Mormon] with such a burden for Nazarene missions!"

Papa died just before Thanksgiving 2000 at the age of 88 after spending his last months in a nursing home. Long after he could no longer hear or see or remember, he spoke blessing to everyone around him. For three evenings before he died, an agency nurse who did not regularly work at the home cared for him. She tended him with great skill and compassion and was there when I sang to him and quoted God's Word and told him how glad I was to be his daughter and his disciple.

The nurse and I were walking down the hall together when she said, "Where do you go to church?" When I told her, she asked if we could accept imperfect people. I assured her we did and gave her directions and my name and number. I could not help thinking that this encounter was a fitting one for the night the "Church Man" went to heaven.

—*Karen Dean Fry*

II—*A God to Glorify*

The Theologian Who Started in a Chicken Coop: J. Kenneth Grider

There is probably no more improbable story than that of J. Kenneth Grider. This retired seminary professor, a member of the committee that translated the *New International Version* of the Bible, was told when he arrived at Olivet Nazarene College that he should go back home.

Stephen S. White, professor of theology at Olivet, encountered the young Grider on the front steps of Burke Administration Building. Grider was dirty, hungry, broke, and out of his cultural element. He had spent 10 days in jail for vagrancy on his way from East St. Louis, Illinois.

But this young man was not going back home. In his heart were the knowledge of sins forgiven, an experience of the sanctifying grace of God, an undeniable call to preach the gospel of Christ, and a faith that God would supply all his needs.

Grider's religious background was varied, haphazard, and anything but scholarly. His mother was a Roman Catholic who taught him to pray to the saints. His father was a Methodist who converted to Catholicism when he wanted to marry his mother. Four years before his conversion experience, Grider had attended a Nazarene revival. The preacher was a Miss Slayball, who married Paul Schwada, who later became dean at Olivet. Kenneth remembers that the singers in the meeting were the Venable sisters.

"Joe," as they called him then, did not really get to know the Nazarenes until his family moved to East St. Louis. There a neighbor lady, Mrs. Largent, a faithful layperson, began to invite the Grider family to the Church of the Nazarene. Every week for eight months, she was faithful either to call or send a note by one of her children inviting the family to church. "Why don't you go, Joe?" his mother asked in the fall of 1939. "She was suggesting that I attend the Fireworks Station Church of the Nazarene in a converted chicken house, which became a basement church and at a later time a basement with a church on top" is the way Dr. Grider described the event. The pastors, Rev. and Mrs. Chester Linton, had not finished high school but had been ordained after passing the course of study.

Joe and his brother, James, attended. The church was in a revival, and when Joe raised his hand for prayer, his brother poked him in the ribs and whispered, "That's a mistake—they'll be after you now!" And they were. The guitar-playing soloist, Albert Mousette, had been watching and praying. After church he said, "I'll be praying for you."

Many people at the little church prayed for him, especially Mrs. Linton. She had felt a leading to go to him to pray for him but told the Lord, "They'll never let me in that house." Nevertheless, she went, they let her in, and she prayed for him. Joe had been praying also, four hours the day before, but he needed help. Mrs. Linton prayed and led him to Christ. Later both of the Lintons helped lead him into the experience of entire sanctification. "They had the wisdom not to guide me to testify to the experience before it had occurred," he explained. "When the experience came, in a weed patch near the parsonage, I hurried to tell them."

The personal experience of being born again, and later sanctified wholly, was the basis for his life of study in the Scriptures and theology. The scholarly degrees and the worldwide respect in scholarly theological circles has not dimmed nor diluted his early knowledge of being "born of the Spirit."

—*L. Wayne Sears*

Radio Pastor to the Whole State of Arkansas: Agnes Diffee

In the days before air conditioning, when you walked down the street of any town in Arkansas between 11 A.M. and noon during the warm-weather months, you would likely hear Agnes Diffee preaching. She held a one-hour service every day during the week and three hours on Sunday on the most powerful and one of the oldest radio stations in Arkansas—KARK.

Agnes Diffee pastored Little Rock First Church from 1931 to 1951. During those 20 years, membership increased from 297 to 1,163. In the *Herald of Holiness,* General Superintendent J. B. Chapman wrote of her effectiveness: "What makes a church grow and succeed? Usually it is difficult to point out any one thing. It is the sum total of many efforts that produce the result. Mrs. Agnes Diffee, pastor of First Church, for example, reported that during the past year she had preached 98 times in the regular Sunday services, 15 in evangelistic services, held 12 outside services in the city, attended 75 prayer meetings, taught a class of young people once a week for 12 weeks, made 700 pastoral calls, attended 12 meetings of executive boards of different organizations, held 12 regular and 5 special meetings of the church board, attended 6 meetings of the ministerial alliance and 2 meetings in behalf of moral issues in the city, had an average of 10 services in the city a week in different institutions, jails, penitentiary, etc., class meetings, prayer meetings, evangelistic services, and radio services."

The long, impressive list continued, and then Chapman added, "I submit that this is an example of a growing, glowing, going church."

Agnes White was born near Pine Bluff, Arkansas, around the turn of the 20th century. While in her teens, she was converted and sanctified in a Holiness revival meeting. A friend recommended she should attend Arkansas Holiness College sponsored by the Church of the Nazarene in Vilonia, Arkansas. That's what she did, paying her school bills working menial jobs. She was a devoted Christian, a good student, and while at Vilonia, she joined the newly organized Nazarene denomination.

Agnes was a tall, attractive woman with an air of confident reserve. She radiated confidence in God and was a sought-after evangelist. During her student days at Arkansas Holiness College, Agnes became acquainted with Roy Diffee. Their friendship ripened into marriage. Though Roy Diffee was never a preacher, he admired his wife and always encouraged her preaching ministry.

The Arkansas District of the Church of the Nazarene granted her a license to preach, and she was ordained as an elder on the Oklahoma District October 26, 1919. For a short time, she and Eupha Beasley, another woman preacher, served as an evangelistic team. Wherever she went, people gladly came to hear her preach.

During this same time period, M. Edward Borders became the pastor of the Church of the Nazarene in Little Rock, Arkansas. He had a magnetic personality; the church took on new life and began to grow under his ministry. He oversaw the construction of a beautiful building. And while radio was in its infancy, he founded station KARK in the mid-1920s. Later when the station was sold, Borders retained one hour of time every day in the week and three hours on Sunday for the church's use. Because of the pressing needs caused by rapid growth, Agnes White Diffee was added to the staff to help carry the heavy workload.

In time, Pastor Borders experienced personal problems unknown to Sister Diffee, and a crisis developed. He took a large part of the congregation and started an independent church some distance away.

At this time, Mrs. Diffee's fortitude and ability were tested when she was asked to serve as pastor. She rose to the occasion, taking over the radio programs and promotional matters of the church. Her preaching and spiritual emphasis were presented in true Nazarene fashion. Love and goodwill abounded. In a few months after a revival meeting or two, hearts and minds were renewed and refreshed, and the church flourished.

Agnes Diffee proved to be a wise pastor and strong leader. God used her to build a large church where she surrounded herself with talented and loyal helpers. Her words of faith and lived-out courage became a source of strength and comfort to many. Little Rock First Church grew until it became the second-largest church in the denomination.

—C. Paul Gray

The Baptist Heretic Who Organized 53 Churches: H. H. Hooker

In the dawning years of the 20th century, the long arm of God reached into the unpromising obscurity of rural Mississippi and found a boy who became a gospel trailblazer and church planter extraordinaire. His name was H. H. Hooker, the year of his birth was 1890, and he grew up on a farm. Through his teens he attended a Baptist church. In 1907 he was converted in a revival held by a Holiness group who later became Nazarenes. On the first Sunday of November in 1908 he preached his first sermon in the Baptist church. The following Saturday he was turned out for preaching "heresy." The next day he joined the Church of the Nazarene. Thus, his ministry and his denomination share the same natal year and almost the same birthday.

Hooker pastored a short while and then attended Peniel College at Peniel, Texas, from 1911 to 1914. He returned to Mississippi for a brief period and then moved in 1915 to the Nauvoo circuit in Alabama, comprised of four churches. In their rubber-tired buggy, an advanced vehicle for that day, he and his wife traveled the country roads of Walker and Winston Counties. Though they had "advanced transportation," they did not have much money. There were days when they had nothing for meals except water, molasses, and cornbread without shortening. Nevertheless, they rejoiced, praised God, and considered the molasses a bonus.

In 1918 Hooker was elected superintendent of the Alabama District. In that same year he received my mother into charter membership of the Church of the Nazarene in Cordova, Alabama. Fifty-six years later he baptized Stuart, our son and my mother's only grandchild at the time—a remarkable span of ministry to one family by one minister.

Hooker served as district superintendent in Alabama until 1928, when he accepted a call to pastor Los Angeles First Church, the mother church of the denomination. He was there 5 years and then returned to Alabama as superintendent from 1933 to 1937. During his 14 years as district superintendent in Alabama, he organized 53 churches, 45 of which were active at his death in 1975.

He conducted most of the initial revivals where these churches were organized.

H. Lamar Smith, pastor of First Church of the Nazarene in Mobile, Alabama, tells of an event that reveals Hooker's unceasing commitment to church planting. During his superintendency in Alabama, he had wanted to organize a church in the port city of Mobile but was unable to do so. After assuming the pastorate in Los Angeles, he did not forget some friends in Mobile who wanted a church there. In 1928, travel from Los Angeles to Mobile was more arduous than travel from Boston to Bombay is today. Still, Hooker sent four men from his Los Angeles congregation to Mobile. After a six-week revival, they organized First Church in Mobile. Two of those four were Fletcher Galloway and Floyd Hawkins. Both men became capable pastors, and Hawkins also became a hymn writer.

Another facet of Hooker's devotion to the good of the church happened in Los Angeles. Pasadena College (now Point Loma Nazarene University) was in a financial crisis; one bank had threatened to close the college and padlock the doors. Pastor Hooker proposed to the congregation of Los Angeles First Church that they mortgage their own debt-free sanctuary and give the money to the college. The church approved the plan, and the college was saved.

Even in retirement, in Gardendale, Alabama, H. H. Hooker continued planting churches. There was no Nazarene church in that suburb of Birmingham, so he became the driving force to organize a church there. Today it is one of the stronger Nazarene congregations in the Birmingham area.

To the present, a quarter century after his death, H. H. Hooker remains the foremost church planter in Alabama Nazarene history. He grew from the doctrinal position of "unconditional security" to the security of the daily witness of the Spirit as he walked with God in holiness of heart and life.

—G. Stuart McWhirter

A Rugged Holiness Preacher with Tender Concern: W. R. Platt

"Holiness should be as beautiful as art, as honest as science, and as vital as life." W. R. Platt of Alabama lived that kind of life. His personal appearance was impeccable—he believed he should exemplify his concern for God's approval of him. He would never have gone to church or to the pulpit in casual dress. Honesty in all things was his watchword. His commitment to Christ allowed nothing of second-rate, halfhearted, spasmodic witness. To him, the vitality of the message of holiness must be all-consuming. That message, revealed to others in every part of his being, meant that Christ is worthy of the best a person can be.

Rev. Platt had the physical appearance to go with his convictions. He was six feet tall and had thick black hair, long sideburns, strong shoulders. His 200 well-distributed pounds told of his careful diet. His shoes were always highly polished, and his car was clean. It was not personal vanity, but a sense of awesome responsibility to represent a holy God, a winsome Jesus, and a searching Holy Spirit that made him give careful attention to his impact upon people.

As a teenager, I was in Rev. Platt's presence on many occasions. Even then I sensed an emanation of strength from him, a kind of warm courage, as from a hidden flame. That warmth and strength I later knew was the presence of the Holy Spirit in his life.

But there was more to him than physical appearance—much more. He was a man of deep convictions. His purpose in life was to "dig out" churches. He "dug out" more churches in Alabama than any other person. Though H. H. Hooker *organized* more Nazarene churches than anyone else in Alabama, W. R. Platt held the revivals and won the people to Christ. Then the district superintendent would organize them.

When Platt felt called of God to go to a new location and start a church, he went. Often he would not know anyone in the community, no one had called him, and no one knew he was coming. There was no advance promotion or survey or committee. It was just W. R. Platt following the leadership of the Holy Spirit. On many occasions he obtained permission from the local sheriff to sleep in the jail. Usually, after a few nights, someone would invite him to stay in his or her home. Often he was hungry. On one occasion, while walking the streets of a town inviting people to come to his "meeting," he prayed, *Lord, I'm hungry. Please help me.* He walked a few steps and saw some change on the sidewalk. A few more steps, and there was more. Soon he had enough for a simple meal. He knew how to pray, *Give us this day our daily bread.*

The vitality of his convictions made Platt fearless. On one occasion he was preaching a home mission revival where there was strong opposition. During one service a man got up, walked up to Rev. Platt, and cursed him publicly. Then the man went out the side door near the pulpit. Platt handed his Bible to his wife, who was also an ordained minister. She continued the sermon while Platt followed the man outside. Just as he caught up with the man, the sheriff came up and said, "It's all right, Preacher. I'll take care of this."

The next day, the sheriff came again and said, "Preacher, this man is dangerous. He's just out of prison. It would be safer for you and your wife if you would leave town."

"Absolutely not," Rev. Platt replied. "The devil did not send me here, and I refuse to let him run me out."

Later the man came back and asked forgiveness. Rev. Platt forgave him, of course, took him back to the church, and preached to him. Even after the man had threatened to do him bodily harm, the preacher was interested in his soul and eternal destiny.

The vitality of the Holiness message gave this minister that fearlessness. He exemplified the maxim "As long as God's hand is upon me, I am immortal." He would knuckle under to no man. When his earlier denomination expelled him for preaching holiness, he went out under the stars in obedience to what he felt was the call of God. His only fear was of God, and that was a reverent fear that had nothing of alarm or terror in it.

In his retirement years, Platt was not content to be the one who "dug out" more churches than anyone else. Out of the meager store of his finances, he continued to give and pray and support the cause of second-blessing holiness that was so dear to his heart and had made him the man he was.

—*Leon Chambers*

Tobacco in the Offering Plate: B. F. Neely

Tobacco—what a strange thing to find in a Nazarene offering plate. A. K. Bracken said a plug of Star Navy chewing tobacco showed up in the offering in a revival in West Texas where B. F. Neely was the evangelist. What kind of person would do this, and why? And what kind of person was the evangelist?

Benjamin Franklin Neely was converted, sanctified, and called to preach after he was married and had a family. Since he had little formal education, he went back to grammar school with some of his children. He soon finished and went on to higher education as opportunity afforded. While rearing his family and furthering his education, he was also busy as an evangelist and pastor and was active in the Texas Holiness Association. This remarkable self-developed man also served as business manager at two Nazarene colleges, as a district superintendent, and held several other positions in the church.

After the 1908 General Assembly, when the church was officially organized at Pilot Point, Texas, Neely was called to return to pastor the church in Peniel, Texas. He took the opportunity to attend classes at the college there.

Among his better-known sermons was one Neely called "Safety First." He used the analogy of a person climbing a tree. If the climber stopped on the bottom limb, and it broke, there was nothing to keep him or her from falling to the ground. It was safer to climb higher, so that if the higher limb broke, he would be saved by the lower branches of the tree.

He would say of those who preached what he called "unconditional security," the teaching that once saved a person can never be lost, "You are on the lowest limb of the tree. If you are wrong, and you do backslide and never return to the Lord, you would be eternally lost. If you are wrong, you are dangerously wrong." Then he would continue: "But if I am wrong, I am harmlessly wrong; for if I cannot fall and be lost, then I am as well off as you are. So if I am wrong, I am harmlessly wrong."

Dr. Neely used the same analogy concerning the second blessing. "If I am wrong, and you are right that it is unattainable,

I am still as well off as you are, so I am harmlessly wrong. But if I am right and you are wrong, and it is true that 'without holiness no man shall see the Lord,' then you are dangerously wrong."

On one of his evangelistic trips, he was traveling from Chattanooga to Nashville. On the train was a zealous advocate of another belief who was going up and down the train challenging people about their churches. This questioner would ask about a person's church, and if, for instance, he or she replied, "Methodist" or "Presbyterian," he would then ask, "Where in the Bible do you find that name?" Arguments ensued, and the questioner, who knew his little limited Bible track well, usually came out best.

Neely knew his turn would come. He knew well the scriptures that the other man asked, but he also knew other parts of the Bible. So when the man got to Neely, Neely asked him questions that he could not answer. A crowd gathered, eager to see what would happen. Neely arose and gave the warm message of full salvation. Dr. Bracken, who told this story, said, "So lost did the questioner become that when the train got to his home station, he did not know it and had to take another train back home. And I doubt if our friend was ever more at home than when he was preaching to that car full of strangers."

Once Neely was conducting a revival in a West Texas town. He had gone into the town without financial backing or congregational sponsorship, found a place, and started a Holiness revival meeting. He always preached his convictions. One of those convictions was the one against tobacco. The Holiness people, many decades before the American Medical Association spoke out against it, regarded the use of tobacco as a self-destroying sin.

At the close of the meeting, Neely had to take his own offering. He told the crowd of his need and had the hat passed. When it came back, some joker had put a plug of chewing tobacco in it. Unperturbed, the old warrior stood before the congregation and counted the money. "Well," he said, "those who had tens put in tens, those who had fives put in fives, those who had dollars put in dollars, those who had cents put in cents—and those who had no sense put in tobacco."

—*L. Wayne Sears*

The Nazarene Will Rogers:
"Uncle Bud" Robinson

"Uncle Bud Robinson," something like the famous Will Rogers, could be an entertaining humorist who made people laugh at the ordinary events of daily living. His true-to-life applications of Scripture, his humor, and his lisp were all used in his unique preaching. A. K. Bracken, longtime president of Bethany-Peniel College, said it succinctly: "You could no more describe nor picture him than you could describe or picture Carlsbad Caverns. To hear his messages and his testimonies—and there was scarcely any difference—was a rare treat. It was easy to sense that he was a living miracle of God's grace."

Reuben A. Robinson was born in a log house in the Cumberland Mountains of eastern Tennessee. Poverty was his heritage, a drinking father his legacy. When his father died, his Presbyterian mother took her brood and moved west to the plains of Texas. Life was hard there. Bud grew up a drinking, fighting cowboy. He could neither read nor write. He suffered with epilepsy and an incurable lisp.

The story of Bud's conversion is remarkable. He said he was a cowboy with a pistol in one pocket and a plug of Star Navy tobacco in the other. Raymond Browning quoted him about his conversion:

That preacher preached on hell until I feared its woe,
And then he preached on heaven until I surely longed to go.

A few years passed before Uncle Bud was sanctified. While he was attending a Holiness camp meeting, conviction seized his soul. His conversion experience had been bright and up to date, but at times he felt the stirrings of the carnal nature. He was working in a cornfield when the blessing came. In his own inimitable way, he described the cornstalks turning gold and Jesus flooding his soul with peace. He often said that Jesus gave him "a hogshead full of honey in my soul, and there's lots of beehives I haven't robbed yet!"

His newfound holiness experience made him unacceptable to some of the leaders of his church. Soon Bud found his home among the Nazarenes and spent the rest of his life with them.

Though Bud was totally illiterate when he was saved, he soon began to remedy that situation. Painstakingly and steadfastly, he learned to read, taking his lessons from the Bible. When he preached, he would go smoothly from one verse to another. Not reading, but reciting, he would say, "Now just hold that verse in your mind, and put this one along with it."

In *Religion, Philosophy, and Fun* he wrote, "The hardest thing I have ever done was to confess Bud Robinson's sins. Gentlemen, I had to nearly sweat blood and just about spit fire, but when I went down a crying and met Jesus, I then came up a flying! The easiest thing I ever have done is confess the other fellow's sins when he wasn't there to listen to me." His writings were mainly didactic, homespun, and inspirational. When he wrote his "Good Samaritan Chats" for the *Herald of Holiness,* he often put a note at the bottom of the manuscript that said, "Here are some periods and commas and other marks. You just use them where you see fit."

In the January 1954 *Preacher's Magazine,* editor James P. McGraw described an incident from his own experience:

> I held the door open while the eighty-year-old evangelist Bud Robinson laboriously climbed into the waiting automobile. He turned his mischievous eyes toward me and remarked dryly, "I used to be able to git on a horse and him a buckin', Brother Jimmy, but now it's about all I kin do to git in a car and it a-standin' still."
>
> The remark he made as he entered the car that evening stayed with me. I think it embodies in a sentence many of the traits of his unique character which made him a successful preacher of the gospel and the best-loved man of his generation. It portrayed humor, kindness, patience, humility, love, and—well, who but "Uncle Bud" could express in such colorful language the thought "I'm not as spry as I once was, so please forgive me for being so slow"?

—*L. Wayne Sears*

Maude, Who Helped Give Our Church a Giant: Maude Frederick Chapman

If a teacher can be judged by the quality of the students he or she produces, then Maude Frederick Chapman must rate near the top of any list of educators. Her pupil was a young, untrained man who was getting started as a preacher by the name of Jimmy Chapman. She was his wife as well as his teacher.

Their son Paul quoted his father as saying that before he met Maude, his grammar was "atrocious." But during his Nazarene ministry as general superintendent, editor, writer, and leader, he became the writer voice of the denomination. He was sometimes called "the Nazarene Socrates" by his contemporaries.

Probably the most lasting influence is his writing. He published more than 6 million words. His source was his prodigious reading. He often read one book per day and then gave the book away to a pastor.

Chapman's preaching was exemplary. His sermons were simple in word but profound in thought. He once said, "The only way some sermons are deep is to stand them up on end."

In all of this, Maude's impact is evident. Chapman's dependence on her was so complete that after she died in February 1940 and he was to preach at the General Assembly in June, he told his son that he thought he had the message but was not sure he could deliver it without her presence. So Paul sat in the auditorium where she usually sat. He said his father often looked at him, but he was seeing Maude. At the close of what many regard as his greatest sermon, "Christ and the Bible," he leaned on the pulpit and wept.

At a district superintendents' conference in Kansas City in June 1946, he preached the message "All Out for Souls." Chapman poured out his heart and soul in an impassioned plea that the church not lose sight of its original goal, the souls of men and women, boys and girls. At the close, again, he leaned over the pulpit and wept. The meeting was electrified. It was like a fresh wind of the Holy Spirit as genuine revival gripped those in attendance.

At his funeral, G. B. Williamson spoke of Abraham Lincoln,

who was known as the great commoner. He likened James Blaine Chapman to Lincoln: anyone could approach him at any time, and everyone did.

His common touch was rooted in his own humble beginnings. Born in southern Illinois on August 20, 1884, he lived the life of a farm boy until he was 14. The family then moved to the Blackjack region of Oklahoma. Blackjack trees are small, dark, hard oak trees that are very tough. To clear the land of them for farming is serious and hard work.

In that region of Oklahoma, "Jimmy" Chapman began his effective ministry. He was converted in a schoolhouse meeting when he was 15. He said he "got saved" in order to get sanctified. The next night after his conversion, he sought and received the blessing of sanctification. From that time on, he began to testify, attend Holiness meetings, and support the Holiness Movement as often as he could. When he was 17, in a schoolhouse meeting east of Noble, Oklahoma, he was testifying and said he felt a "thumb in his back" impelling him to the front of the platform. He took that as a confirmation of his call to preach and began immediately to prepare for his work.

At the age of 17, he met Maude Frederick, a young schoolteacher. She, too, had recently been sanctified and was attending every meeting she could while teaching. She was 21 years old and well-educated for the time. Jimmy Chapman was asked to take her to a train so she could return to her teaching assignment. This was the first time they had been alone together. At the station, Jimmy felt the Lord say, "There is your future wife." Soon after that, in the presence of others, with no courtship, Jimmy asked her to marry him. When she refused, he began in private to ask the Lord to forgive her for not obeying the will of God. One year later, at about the same place and in the same group of friends, he again proposed—and she accepted.

The couple were married in Blossom, Texas, February 18, 1903, by C. B. Jernigan. Jimmy preached that night, and the next day they went to Indian Territory to begin another revival. His education began immediately, with grammar and English. Soon afterward the Chapmans moved to Vilonia, Arkansas, for him to study Greek, English, and theology. He completed the course in two years.

In 1911 the couple moved to the Holiness university at Peniel, Texas, where his later longtime friend and coworker R. T. Williams was president. Here he earned his bachelor of divinity degree in one year. In 1912 he was made dean of the university and earned his bachelor of arts degree. In 1913 he followed Williams as president of Peniel University. Later, when he left the presidency of the university to pastor the church in Bethany, Oklahoma, Chapman assumed the entire indebtedness of the small school. He paid on that debt most of his life. When it was finally paid, he told Maude, "Now we can begin to get some of the things for the home that you've always wanted." She replied, "We've done without them this long, and the missionaries need lots of things too."

Along with problems of long journeys, weary days, and burdens of the church, there came two personal and tragic losses. Their son, Brillheart, died in New York City under tragic circumstances. Then, after 37 years of marriage, Maude was stricken with pneumonia and died. The loss of his companion, teacher, and sweetheart was devastating. Their life's burdens were beginning to ease, and years of continued service lay ahead.

After a few years, Louise Robinson, missionary to Africa, married Dr. Chapman. She was a blessing to him as she had been to others all her life.

G. B. Williamson said of Chapman: "He was a man of such unusual capacities that any given group of people can only hope to have one in a hundred years. Indeed, it is too much to expect that ever again a man possessed of all his gifts and graces shall be given to us." His assessment seems accurate to this day.

Praise the Lord for the influence of a woman like Maude Frederick Chapman, who truly gave the church and the Holiness Movement a giant unlike any other.

—*L. Wayne Sears*

A Holiness Preacher Who
Walked the Talk: David Monroe Coulson

David Monroe Coulson was a pioneer preacher in the Church of the Nazarene. He was a tall Texan with piercing blue eyes. His last years were spent on the old Florida District, and that's when I came to know him. I was his pastor for a year before he died, and he loved to visit the parsonage and talk about his ministry.

When he was a boy, he stood with his father on the bank of a wide river. "How far is it to the other side?" his father asked.

"I don't know," the lad replied.

"That's a good answer, Son," his father said. "Never be ashamed of admitting you don't know something."

Coulson never pretended a knowledge he didn't possess. He was honestly humble and humbly honest.

He pioneered the cause of holiness in New York City with C. B. Jernigan. They stretched a tent between two tall buildings, and in the summer the canvas was quite hot. One afternoon Coulson removed his coat while preaching. A woman, upset by this, arose and started to leave. "Just a moment, Sister," Coulson called out. She stopped in the sawdust aisle, her back to him. "You are offended because I removed my coat. I am still clothed from my Adam's apple down to my wrists and ankles. But when you turned from me, I could see the fifth joint in your backbone. Now you sit down and listen while I finish this sermon." The woman dropped like a beanbag into the nearest seat and listened attentively to the rest of his sermon.

Coulson came to the Southeast as pastor of our "mother church" in the area, Donalsonville, Georgia. He met weekly with the pastors of the Baptist and Methodist churches of that town. One morning he walked in on a red-hot argument about water baptism. Said the Methodist, "If I baptize a man all but his head, is that a valid baptism?"

"No," said the Baptist. "He has to go clear under the water."

"What if I dip him up to his hairline—is that a valid baptism?"

"No, he has to go clear under."

"That proves it," exclaimed the Methodist. "It's the water on top of his head that constitutes real baptism!"

At that point, the disputants actually came to blows, and Coulson had to physically separate them.

He could do it. He was a strong and courageous man. Once when he was conducting a tent revival in a Midwestern town, a local ruffian took umbrage at Coulson's attack on whiskey. The angry man met Coulson in the middle of the street, whipped out a knife, and threatened to cut his heart out. Coulson quietly demanded, "Give me the knife." The man finally handed it over and slunk away. Coulson told me, "I would step into any kind of danger for the gospel's sake."

D. M. Coulson was a practical man. He wore dentures and carried a spare set in his pocket. He explained to me, "I have a lightweight set for preaching and a heavier set for chewing solid food." He was preaching at the Suwannee River Church in north Florida one Sunday morning when his dentures popped out of his mouth. He caught them in midair, slipped them into his coat pocket, and never missed a word of his message.

He lived for his message, and his message was holiness. He once told me that in 60 years of preaching, he had never addressed a message to sinners—he always preached to the church. "But hundreds of sinners got under conviction and found the Lord in my services," he added.

At Sparr, Florida, one morning when Coulson walked into a grocery store, the owner said to some cronies, "Here's that Holiness preacher. He thinks you can be perfect." Coulson walked to a corner and took a broom and swept the floor. "This is a perfect broom," he said. "It does what it is intended to do." He continued: "This is a perfect watch. It keeps time. The Bible tells us to be perfect, and that means doing what God created us to do. He created us to love Him with all our heart and our neighbor as ourselves. That's what holiness means."

When he had not been seen for a day, a neighbor went by to see him and found him on the floor. He had fallen and broken his leg. He was saying, "Praise the Lord! Glory to God!" When asked how he could do that, he replied, "I've got two legs, and the other one isn't broken!"

On his deathbed at the age of 90, his last words were, "It is

glory." His last sermon was from 2 Cor. 4:17: "For our light afflic-
tion, which is but for a moment, worketh for us a far more ex-
ceeding and eternal weight of glory" (KJV). He was exchanging the
afflictions of earth for the glories of heaven.

Men and women of Coulson's love, faith, courage, and integrity poured their lives into the foundations of our church.

—*William. E. McCumber*

From One Conversion Came 19 Christian Workers: John N. Nielson

As a young lad of 10, John N. Nielson was playing one Sunday when a lady invited him to Sunday School at a Holiness
church. He began attending regularly. When he was 11 or 12 years
old, he saw a young girl go forward in a revival meeting and pro-
fess salvation. He said to himself, "If she can do that, I can too."
He sought the Lord on successive nights and finally received the
assurance that he, too, was born again.

When he became a young man, he joined that church, the
Holiness Christian Church. It was part of a small denomination
that united with the Church of the Nazarene in 1908 under the
leadership of Horace and Jonas Trumbauer. After marrying a
pretty girl he met in that church in 1915, he soon felt called to
preach. Not disobedient, he gave up a career in accounting and in
1916 accepted the pastorate of the Church of the Nazarene in
Darby, Pennsylvania. That started a journey of more than 50
years of ministry during which he served as pastor, district superintendent, and evangelist.

John B. Nielson, one of his sons who became adult editor for
Nazarene Sunday School publications, wrote, "The family still
honors that unknown woman who invited a small lad to Sunday
School. Some 85 years have passed, and from that one conversion
has come three minister sons, one daughter who is a minister's
wife, another daughter an Eastern Nazarene College professor and
professor's wife, three ministers' wives nieces, two nephew minis-

ters, five minister grandsons, and four great-grandchildren in full-time Christian service. From Philadelphia to Boston, to Kansas, Alabama, Texas, Michigan, Illinois, Ohio, Maryland, New York, and Vermont, to Europe from Finland to Sicily, Israel, and England, that unknown lady's influence goes on for Christ and His Church. And the end is not yet. Someday our family expects to see that woman in heaven and thank her for inviting a little boy by the name of John N. Nielson—my father—to Sunday School."

Being a district superintendent, Nielson had to travel a large area by train and would be gone for weeks at a time. Our mother, the remarkable lady he married, was left to manage the family on a meager income. Alone, she had to care for five small children with space heaters and no running water. She drove the 1918 Model T Ford, raised a garden and chickens, and made clothes for her children.

When Nielson resigned from the Washington-Philadelphia District to help his wife in rearing their children, the children understood that for their father, position and career in the church took second place to his responsibilities to win his family to Christ.

One of the brightest memories of the family is of their father as a man of prayer. His son Joseph wrote,

My father was a "man of prayer," a "straight arrow," and known as a man of God. His demeanor was forthright but always kind and gentle. Even with these characteristics, he was human. When he was pastoring the Lowell, Massachusetts, church, the core of the congregation consisted of old-time Methodists. They still observed the Wesley class meeting. A layman led the meeting in song and exhorted from the Scriptures. One night, John Nielson was blessed and sang the chorus, "I Love Him." He had his hand raised, his head back, and his bass voice at its best. He sang, "I love Him, I love Him, because He first loved me. I hear those gentle voices calling, . . ." Then he lapsed into the secular song by Stephen Foster that uses the same melody.

Prayer and life, spiritual and secular, lofty and human were all part of the holy man who has so impacted the church through his family to this day.

—*Joseph F. Nielson, as told to L. Wayne Sears*

III—*To Serve the Present Age*

Mother Was a Preacher
Who Loved Ruffles and Bows: Estelle Crutcher

My mother, Estelle Crutcher, felt called to preach just after World War I. A woman preacher in 1929 was almost unheard of and usually not welcomed. In spite of those cultural complications, the Church of the Nazarene opened its doors to those courageous few who literally became trailblazers. As I listened many times to Mother's life story, I often thought she was one of the most unlikely candidates for such an unusual calling.

Her parents were independent missionaries in northern India from 1892 to 1912. During those years, they had a son and two daughters. Mother was the middle child, born in 1898. Being extremely competitive, highly motivated, and stubbornly domineering, she refused to recognize any limitations. She received her formal education at a boarding school in the foothills of the Himalayan Mountains where the classes were strictly disciplined and advanced in the British system of education. She received highest honors as well as an all-India scholarship for pianoforte.

When she was 14, the family moved to a farm in Canada, her mother's birthplace. She never adjusted to farm life and longed for more education. Eventually her parents made plans for her to attend God's Bible School in Cincinnati, Ohio. But she was turned back at the United States border because she was underage. In her anger, frustration, and disappointment, she backslid and became hostile toward God and religion.

When she was 18, she met my father, a handsome, English-born soldier in the Canadian Army. Against her parents' wishes and in a backslidden state, she married him. She followed her new husband to London, and there during World War I in a little 900-year-old village outside London, with air raids screaming and bombs falling, I, the first of her six children, was born to this frightened and lonely young wife.

Mother was a true original. My father, a sergeant-major who lived through unspeakable horrors in the trenches of France, was wounded and sent back to England. In time, we moved back to Canada, where my sister was born. My father found work in the United States on the Northern-Pacific Railroad, and we moved to St. Paul, Minnesota. Neither my mother nor my father knew the Lord at that time.

But my grandmother's prayers were unfaltering for her rebellious daughter. While the family was in St. Paul, my brother was born prematurely. When mother held her firstborn son in her arms and realized he might not live, she promised God to return to her faith if He would spare her child. In His loving mercy, God spared him, and mother never again wavered from her commitment. But she had a way to go as she soon realized her besetting sin was a hot temper. She sought the second blessing in her little St. Paul kitchen and later testified that she walked the floor and, suffused with joy, cried over and over, "He has come! He has come!" and glory filled her soul.

After some time, she began to feel a possible call to preach. She prayed in true distress of soul as she realized her obstacles. She had three children and a husband who was not interested in religion. How could this be from God? She went to a godly minister for counsel, and he wisely advised her to say yes and await God's open doors. I believe the minister helped God open a door. Soon she was asked to speak in an afternoon camp meeting—her first sermon at age 24. She made notes diligently, studied, and prayed. When she got up to preach, a brisk wind blew her notes away. Not hesitating, she left them on the floor and preached freely without notes. For over 50 years of ministry, she never used a note—she hid the Word in her heart and let the Holy Spirit unfold the truth clearly and with anointing.

Later she enrolled in the home course of study, and in spite of the demands of home and family, she became ordained in her early 30s. My mother was very feminine in the pulpit. Being of French descent, she liked ruffles and frills, perfumes, perky bows, and bright colors. But after some time she felt more comfortable in a clerical robe. Her constant theme was holiness. Her approach was logical and always scriptural.

For us as a family, there were few "clouds of glory," probably more clouds of confusion, as we followed in her train. But we never doubted her devotion to Christ. Her love for us was complete, and she never apologized for our way of life. Eventually, her long-suffering husband was saved, and all her children became productive adults.

What more shall I say? There's not space to write of her exploits of faith, the numbers of people she helped to find the Lord, and the many for whom she opened up the way into the abundant life of sanctification. My mother lived life to the full for nearly 98 years. In the paraphrased words of an old saint, I feel she "steered through every storm with a fervent intent and steadfast courage and a trust fixed on God."

—Hazel C. Lee

He Passed the Torch: R. W. Cunningham

As the music faded, R. W. Cunningham rose to conduct the chapel service at the West Virginia South Nazarene Bible College Extension in South Charleston, West Virginia. The students opened each chapel service by singing "wonderful, wonderful, Jesus is to me!" It was Dr. Cunningham's favorite chorus and represented the center of his life.

Dr. Cunningham was elected to serve as director of the Bible college extension in 1986, a position he held until he retired at the age of 95. At a time in life when many educators would have retired, he had continued to give faithful service.

On November 26, 1989, Pastor Morton Estep and South Charleston First Church of the Nazarene honored Dr. Cunningham's 70 years in Christian ministry by dedicating their new Family Life Center to him. He received greetings and congratulations from hundreds of people throughout North America whose lives he had blessed.

Raymond W. Hurn, who had worked with Dr. Cunningham, wrote, "Our entire church is honored by the life you have lived, the consistency of your Christian witness and ministry, and the love of God that has been shown so clearly in all of your labors."

R. W. Cunningham graduated form Nyack and Malone colleges. After a career of pastoring in Ohio, he came in 1949 with his wife and two small sons, Barry and Raymond, to pastor a predominantly Black Nazarene congregation in Institute, West Virginia, just west of South Charleston.

The General Assembly in 1944 made long-range plans to give the Black churches of North America a place to train evangelists and other Christian workers. Institute was chosen as the site.

The school became known as Nazarene Bible Institute. Dr. Cunningham followed E. E. Hale, the first president, as director soon after the organization was underway. The school was under the auspices of the Department of Home Missions and Evangelism and particularly targeted the Black ministers in the southern districts.

In 1970 the school merged with Nazarene Bible College at Colorado Springs. After the closing of the school, the need for some informal Bible classes for ministers became apparent, and classes were soon organized and conducted at the Institute Church of the Nazarene. The teacher—R. W. Cunningham.

In 1986 the West Virginia South Nazarene Bible College Extension opened with classes conducted in a wing of First Church of the Nazarene in nearby South Charleston. Dr. Cunningham was named director. The aim was still to educate ministerial students so that regardless of whether God called them to serve the intellectual elite or the mentally challenged, their messages would be filled with heart-lifting words of compassion.

It is said that Dr. Cunningham influenced more Black men and women in the preparation for the ministry than any other man. However, he believed that Black students did not want to be "separate and equal," that a better approach in recruiting students was to treat all the same, regardless of race. He carried out this philosophy so well that all his students loved and respected him.

On one occasion Dr. Cunningham was in our home and noticed a handmade chest that had been in the family for three generations. He said it reminded him of his work as a young man in a furniture factory when he found a dilapidated old chair in the trash. He took the chair into the shop, reinforced the weak joints, sanded and polished the rough surfaces, and covered the stains with new upholstery. When finished, the chair was beautiful and ready to be used for many years to come.

How like his work in educating men and women for the ministry! He strengthened their weak places, polished their rough edges, and fitted them for long service in God's kingdom.

Dr. Cunningham's students remember him with pleasure and still quote him. When they were discouraged, he often asked them, "Are you on top of the world, or is the world on top of you?" When he presented a deep doctrinal discourse, he would suggest that they "cognate on that for a while." For steadfastness he cautioned, "Be good to your conscience, and your conscience will be good to you" and "Develop and hold your convictions strong, and in time of temptation your convictions will hold you."

None of his students will forget his closing chapel prayer from the Psalms: "Let the words of my mouth, and the meditation of my heart, be acceptable in thy sight, O LORD, my strength, and my redeemer" (Ps. 19:14, KJV).

How do you measure the worth of an ordinary man? By his bank account, his stock portfolio, the size of his house, or the make of his car? Hardly. R. W. Cunningham would not score very high in those categories. His greatest reward was to see his students grow in grace and to know that he passed the torch to them, helping them achieve success in their God-called field of service. And that made him rich in joyful satisfaction.

—*Elsie J. Ours*

A Broken Window Brings
Light to Knight: John L. Knight

God used a broken window to open a new world to John L. Knight. It happened in 1919, soon after his family of two parents and eight children moved in a horse-drawn wagon to Mineral Wells, Texas. They were blessed by settling near a family with a great heart and tolerant spirit.

Here's how the relationship started. The Knight boys were playing ball in their yard. Whether it was a wild pitch or a foul ball, the ball broke the neighbors' window. The boys ran for cover. Later, when their father went to pay for the window, the neighbor refused money and invited the Knight family to the Church of the Nazarene.

Almost immediately Johnny Lee Knight, who had been converted earlier in a Baptist church, began to attend regularly, and the Nazarenes lovingly received him. Fifty years later, there is still a contingent of the Knight family active in many phases of the Mineral Wells church.

In 1919 the Church of the Nazarene was only 11 years old. The pastor at Mineral Wells was Rev. Greer. He was a strong supporter of the church's ministry on the district and general levels. His newest church member, Johnny Lee, learned early to follow that pattern. He soon joined the church and quickly became a youth leader. He served on the church board, and after he became a pastor, he loved to testify that he had filled every position in that church except missionary society president and pianist.

During those days an evangelistic team came to the church. He fell in love with and married one of them, Beulah Bounds. She left the evangelistic team and joined him in organizing a new family team.

Soon after their marriage, John felt called to preach. With only a fourth grade education and a new wife and family to support, he found it difficult to accept. Working as a butcher in a meat market, he faithfully served his church and completed the four-year course of study in two and a half years. He was then called to pastor the Mineral Wells church and began a 55-year ministry.

Knight served the Church of the Nazarene in many assignments. He served for 8 years as pastor, 22 years as district superintendent of two districts, 6 years as secretary of evangelism for the denomination, and the remaining years as an evangelist. Well beyond retirement age, during the last year of his ministry he conducted 42 revivals, loving the pastors and laypeople and giving his all to help advance the church.

His appointment as superintendent of the Florida District was a great challenge to him. The district consisted of 47 churches. His strong commitment to starting new congregations led to the establishment of a Home Missions Revolving Fund for the purpose of purchasing property and lending money to new congregations to construct buildings. In 1960, the fund had grown to several hundred thousand dollars, a huge amount for that day. In only one year during that time, 14 new churches were organized.

His burden for souls caused him to propose and organize a district camp program. The old Suwannee Campground became a spiritual haven for people of all ages.

When he closed his ministry as Florida district superintendent, he left over 100 active churches, and the district was eventually reorganized for even greater growth into three districts. A time of tough decision came when he was called to lead the Department of Evangelism. His strong denominational loyalty dictated that he accept the position, but in whatever service assignment he took, he was always a strong evangelist who preached the doctrine of perfect love.

Like many of our early leaders, John L. Knight was a strong personality not without critics. It was said by a few that when he left Florida, "Florida is now heaven—there's no Knight there." Earlier, after serving as the superintendent of the Abilene District, he was not reelected. Another man, W. B. Walker, was elected in his place. When the final ballot was cast and Rev. Walker was elected district superintendent, Knight rose from his seat by the side of the presiding general superintendent, R. T. Williams, met Rev. Walker halfway up the aisle, and extended to him a warm hand of fellowship and congratulations. Dr. Williams remarked, "Holiness works when you've got it!" That's exactly what John L. Knight tried to preach and live.

—Marselle Knight

A College Dean for
All Seasons: Carl S. McClain

When the Holy Spirit looks upon a group of people who are sincerely seeking to advance the kingdom of God, He also looks on into their future and develops the kinds of leaders they will need. Carl S. McClain arrived on the campus of Olivet Nazarene College as a shy, backward boy of 16 who was a high school freshman. Fifty-seven years later, he retired from active service at the college, having served every administrative position in the college except president and dean of women.

He is best remembered for the 22 years he served as academic dean. That period spanned the service years of five different college presidents: T. W. Willingham, A. L. Parrott, Grover Van Dyne, Selden Kelley, and Harold W. Reed. That in itself was a remarkable accomplishment, made possible by his quiet, gentle trust in God. He was always there like the gyroscope in the hold of an ocean liner to provide balance. Through those 22 years, directions varied, controversies arose, and personalities clashed, but the academic purpose of the college stayed on an even keel. Young people were trained, the message of holiness went forth, and the quiet influence of Carl McClain kept "Old Zion comin' through."

When Dr. McClain became dean, there was no one on the faculty with more than a master's degree. To improve the situation, he developed ties with the University of Illinois. Faculty development programs and professional studies were instituted. In 1948 he initiated the first step toward regional accreditation, which was finally accomplished in 1956.

Early in the time of his teaching, in 1933, he instituted a debate team. Immediately the team began to attend tournaments. In 1939 the Illinois Intercollegiate League awarded two trophies at the conclusion of the state meet, one trophy for the best affirmative team and the other for the best negative team. Olivet won them both.

McClain's first love was for his students. He taught at least one course each of his 51 years on the faculty. On his desk he had a plate that said to his students, "You are my business"—not that they did not at times take advantage of his mild manner. One Halloween night, the back stoop of his house that furnished access to the rear door somehow managed to walk across the street and into the center of the campus. He knew more than his students imagined, so he approached the four culprits one at a time and asked if they would be willing to help him bring the steps back. All readily agreed, only to find that they were the only four asked to help. When he offered to pay for their services, they declined. So they moved the stoop twice—for nothing except red faces and the realization that they were the ones who were embarrassed.

Carl McClain was a quiet, gentle man unruffled by circumstances. He had a wealth of common sense and was by nature a peacemaker. When asked to present in writing his philosophy of life, he emphasized two guidelines: (1) endeavor to see yourself as others see you, and (2) endeavor to see others as they see themselves. He learned to take an attitude of suspended judgment concerning the actions, character, and Christian experience of others.

His gifts and faithfulness were recognized by the church. He served as an elected lay delegate to seven general assemblies. In 1957 he was awarded the first layman's "O" award by Olivet. In 1960 the General Assembly gave him a citation of merit that read, "In grateful recognition of meritorious service to youth through the medium of Christian higher education."

Scripture teaches that "the steps of a good man are ordered by the LORD: and he delighteth in his way" (Ps. 37:23, KJV). Here the "delight" comes from both persons. Carl McClain delighted in the way of the Lord—and the Lord delighted in Carl's way.

—*Barbara McClain Bloom*

They Met at the Altar Twice: J. Erben and Altha Moore

They first met when each went to an old-fashioned mourner's bench in September 1908. She was 16-year-old Altha Westmoreland at one end of the altar, and he was 18-year-old Erben Moore at the other end of the altar. They did not receive complete victory that night but kept seeking. Altha was praying in her dormitory at Arkansas Holiness College in Vilonia, Arkansas, for salvation the night of October 15 when the president of the college, Rev. C. L. Hawkins, came in and said, "Miss Altha, you've been seeking the Lord for some time. You told the Lord you would do anything He wanted you to do if He would save you. Won't you just give me your hand, and as you do, turn your life over into the Lord's hands? Let Him be responsible for showing you what to do."

Altha extended her hand, and as she did, she quietly surrendered her life to God and accepted His unconditional love and forgiveness. Three days later, on October 18, Erben Moore received a similar assurance of victory.

At about the same time, on October 13, 1908, the Church of the Nazarene came into being at Pilot Point, Texas. Two more weeks passed, and Rev. James B. Chapman came to Vilonia to pastor what had become the Church of the Nazarene. Soon Chapman preached a sermon on sanctification, speaking about the 11-day journey from the Red Sea to Kadesh-Barnea, where the Israelites should have crossed into Canaan. Altha went to the altar seeking to be sanctified. A Free Methodist pastor, Meda Burnapp, prayed with her, quoting the promise, "If we walk in the light . . . the blood of Jesus Christ his Son cleanseth us from all sin" (1 John 1:7, KJV). Altha willingly believed, and the Holy Spirit witnessed to her surrendered will. Erben had been sanctified three days earlier. Her salvation experience came three days before his, he was sanctified three days before she was, and they were three years apart in age (he was three years older).

In the spring of 1909 Altha had to return to her home near Prescott, Arkansas, because her parents could no longer afford the $14.50 monthly expense. Her habits of prayer and Bible reading soon brought about a revival, and a Nazarene church was organized that included her family.

By 1911 Altha was 19 years old and had returned to Arkansas Holiness College, staying in the J. B. Chapman home, caring for the children and attending school. Erben was also helping out in the Chapman home, milking the cows and doing other work for his room and board. Erben and Altha were married May 29, 1912, on the lawn of the Chapman home. Erben was ordained an elder by General Superintendent Phineas F. Bresee in 1914.

Both Rev. and Mrs. Moore were influenced by the Old Main Spring Camp near Prescott, Arkansas, from the time of their childhood. Other well-known leaders from that camp included A. Milton Smith, W. T. White, Rufus Cummings, and Horace Honea. Erben pastored, evangelized, served as district superintendent, and was always a friend to young pastors. He led some of our largest Nazarene churches, in Houston; Dallas; and Wichita, Kansas. He was host pastor when the General Assembly was held in Wichita in 1932.

This couple, whose lives were so intertwined with the beginnings of the Church of the Nazarene, served faithfully for 65 years. Their children followed in their footsteps. Their son Mark R. Moore served as pastor, district superintendent, and college president. After he was 70, he helped establish African Nazarene College in Kenya. Grandchildren and great-grandchildren have followed Erben and Altha's lead as well.

A humorous thing happened in Erben's early days at Vilonia that tells much about the social isolation in which he grew up. One day at the long dormitory breakfast table at the college in Vilonia, he was seated at the end. As a teenager from a farm, he had never heard of Grape-Nuts cereal. After prayer, he began to pour the cereal onto his plate. Of course, many of them jumped off the plate and scattered. The matron came to the red-faced boy and said, "Mr. Moore, pour the Grape-Nuts in your bowl and add sugar and cream." That was his first experience with "citified" cereal.

If you wonder about Vilonia, Arkansas, its location is so widely unknown that when Evangelist Charles Hastings Smith was asked, "Where in the world is Vilonia, Arkansas?" he replied, "It's about a mile the other side of 'Resume Speed.'" But the Moores and many other early Holiness leaders began there.

—*Roxie Ann Moore Wessels*

U.S. Parole Board Chairman Who Took God as His Senior Partner: George Reed

The chairman of the United States Board of Parole was under extreme pressure in 1971. The president of the United States, Richard M. Nixon, and U.S. Attorney General John Mitchell wanted him to recommend that Teamster president Jimmy Hoffa be released from prison. Mitchell's concern was for Nixon's reelection, which needed the Teamsters' influence and financial support. Mitchell's parting barb to the chairman was, "Your board will follow your lead, George, if you support Hoffa's release."

George Joseph Reed, a longtime member of the Church of the Nazarene, was that chairman. It was clear that unless Hoffa was paroled, Reed's standing with the president and Attorney General Mitchell would be nearly nonexistent. After long self-examination, a "still, small voice" said, "Fear God, but fear no man." So George Reed chose the path of obedience to God. During the decision process, George was reminded of Joseph, who trusted God and defied Pharaoh.

Where was this monumental courage rooted in George Reed? What helped him to choose principle over expediency in his hour of crisis?

Go back a few years. George, with his brothers Harold, Edwin, and Wesley, attended a one-room school in Dundy County, Nebraska. Their teacher, Miss Fly Offin, taught them reading, writing, arithmetic, and faith in God. From her they learned that the Ten Commandments and "liberty under law" were foundation stones of America.

"Liberty under law" was brought into even sharper focus in Colorado Springs when George was in high school. He had been staying out late and racing the family Model A Ford, which brought his father's intense negative reaction. When George invited his girlfriend to the junior-senior banquet, he was told, "You can't have the car tonight." The "law" curtailed his liberty, and he and his girl had to walk to the banquet. Then it rained and spoiled her pretty dress! Later, George observed that "liberty under law" fortified him for the time when he would bear serious responsibility in hundreds of federal cases, including those of such infamous federal prisoners as John Mitchell, Jimmy Hoffa, the Bird Man of Alcatraz, and Alger Hiss.

George Reed's leadership ability was evident during student days at Pasadena College (now Point Loma Nazarene University), as an officer in the U.S. Navy, as regional director for the California Youth Authority, and as deputy director of the Minnesota Youth Conservation Commission. Finally, he was appointed by President Eisenhower and confirmed by the U.S. Senate to the U.S. Board of Parole, where he served for 23 years under five presidents.

Reed crossed a spiritual "Rubicon"—a decisive, irrevocable step—in Minnesota before being named to the parole board. He was teaching a Sunday School class of young married couples at Minneapolis First Church of the Nazarene. That year Sunday School Editor in Chief Albert Harper had written a 13-Sunday series of lessons in the Nazarene adult curriculum on entire sanctification. Reed said of his own spiritual status, "Because of my background in criminology and behavioral psychology, I had convinced myself I could not understand the doctrine of sanctification." His error, of course, was giving more attention to social sciences than to Scripture. Now he faced a real test of personal integrity. By the time the third lesson came, "Experiencing Heart Holiness," he became more convicted of his need for a holy heart. He said, "I felt naked as I attempted to explain what I had not experienced."

Reed continued: "I felt like a fraud before those who trusted me and respected me. I broke out in a sweat. I rushed from the room, feeling I was an utter failure. Drained. Exhausted."

The next morning Reed headed for his office, but the burden became unbearable. So he turned off the highway and stopped. Then he broke into sobs in a prayer of confession. "I felt there was nothing George Reed couldn't do. Now all my illusions were swept away. In response to that inner voice that said, 'Why don't you let me take full charge of your life?' I responded, 'Yes, Lord—I surrender George Reed to You from this hour and forever.' At that moment, I knew the Holy Spirit had become my 'Senior Partner' for life."

About the position of power and trust on the parole board, George Reed observed, "Only as I was subject to God's authority could I act wisely and fairly in exercising the grave responsibility entrusted to me."

"Fear no man" was in sharp focus in Reed's mind when Attorney General Mitchell was pushing for James Hoffa's release. The board rejected the request. However, President Nixon later took the matter into his own hands and signed an executive grant of clemency, making Hoffa eligible for immediate release. Did the forces of evil prevail? Not so. After Watergate, John Mitchell himself came before the board for a hearing. Who did he face? George Reed.

After reading Reed's autobiography, *Fear No Man,* Senator Mark Hatfield wrote, "George Reed has lived an extraordinary life with extraordinary consequences. *Fear No Man* includes fascinating vignettes of his public and private life with a steady dose of spiritual inspiration. His call for a spiritual awakening is one this country should heed."

—*Evelyn Sutton*

IV—My Calling to Fulfill

The Commoner Who Saved Trevecca from Ruin: A. B. Mackey

A. B. Mackey, beloved longtime president of Trevecca Nazarene College, now University, loved to make statements that shocked his hearers. In a district assembly he said there were more hypocrites around a Holiness church than anywhere else. The presiding general superintendent, H. V. Miller, challenged his statement. With a twinkle in his eye, Mackey turned to the assembly audience and said, "Pardon me, folks, while I explain things to the general."

This remarkable man was tall and lanky, somewhat like Abe Lincoln. Like Lincoln, he was full of good humor, wise, distinctly individual, with family roots in Kentucky. Mackey was born April 16, 1897, on a hillside farm adjoining Ill-Will Creek in Clinton County, Kentucky. His father died when he was one year old, leaving Mariba Mackey with seven children. In Kentucky and throughout the South, life was especially difficult. The results from the Civil War were part of daily life. But for a widow with a large family, just daily existence was all but impossible. Typical of the hardy pioneer stock, they survived and made surprising headway against impossible odds.

The history of Trevecca, like other early Holiness schools, is one of heroic faith and frequent near-fatal difficulties. Though the Church of the Nazarene has eight strong liberal arts colleges in the United States, many of the earlier colleges did not survive. Those that did were the results of men like Mackey who faced the lack of money, prestige, and standing in the community and somehow by faith and desperate sacrifice managed to stay alive.

An excerpt from Mackey's Founders' Day address of November 13, 1959, tells in graphic language about one event that could have destroyed the college. In the summer of 1934, during the depths of the Great Depression, Trevecca College lost her beautiful campus on Gallatin Road in Nashville to her creditors; so quarters were rented in a building on the bluff of the Cumberland River in Kentucky for two years. Speaking of that time, Dr. Mackey told the chapel audience,

During that summer, I was left with the responsibility of moving the school to the old campus of Kingswood College in Kentucky. I didn't understand all about it. I went over there and looked at the place. I traveled by bus to the nearest bus station, and then I walked four miles out a dusty road— no gravel, no hard surface road—for four miles. Out there in the middle of the tobacco section of the county, I found an old, ramshackled tabernacle and several old buildings. They were ready to fall down—fire traps at the best.

As I walked back on that dusty road to the bus station, I counted my money, and I didn't have enough to get to Nashville. "Well," I said, "that fixes it. Trevecca College is dead, and I can't do anything about it, and I might as well go back to my home in Kentucky and forget all about it." Well, I bought a ticket to my hometown, Highway, but I hadn't ridden very far until I felt like Jonah on his way to Nineveh. I could see that old whale halfway to me with his mouth open to swallow me. I don't know what all I saw, but I turned to the Lord and said, "Yes, but I don't even have money to get back."

Well, there was a kind of suggestion: "Would you be willing to go back if you did have it?" But I said, "I don't have it, and I wouldn't want to be begging." I had never stooped to that. Something impelled me to check with the driver. I checked with the driver of the bus and asked him the fare to Nashville, and he quoted me the price that it would take to extend my ticket to Nashville, and, lo and behold, I had the money. I don't know how that happened. I don't know what had come about, but I had enough money to buy my ticket to Nashville and exactly seven cents that would pay my streetcar fare back to the little store on North First Street, 20 feet long and 18 feet wide, in which was stored the entire remains of Trevecca Nazarene College.

I came back to Nashville, and what happened I don't understand yet. Nobody blamed me; nobody ever praised me. . . . Anyway, we didn't move to that old campus out there four miles from nowhere.

Here Dr. Mackey might have told another one of his stories. He would sometimes say, "I've held every job at Trevecca from janitor down to president. There's just about as much dishonor in it as honor. Like Abe Lincoln's story about the man being ridden out of town on a rail, 'If it weren't for the honor of the thing, I'd just as soon walk.'"

Just four years after this, in 1938, President Mackey announced to a startled faculty a goal: "On to a four-year college and a million-dollar campus." The idea caught on, and the first class receiving A.B. degrees graduated in 1942. The million-dollar campus became a reality a few years later.

A. B. Mackey served as president for 27 years, saw six major buildings constructed, built a stable institution, and retired in 1963, leaving Trevecca virtually debt-free. This intriguing teacher, able administrator, and loyal churchman died in 1973.

—*Homer J. Adams*

————— ⋈ —————

A True Pioneer Who Gave More than 50 Years on the Front Line: Emma Irick

Years ago it was reported that a "fistfight" nearly took place at a truck stop near Lufkin, Texas. It started when one trucker made unkind remarks about women preachers. Another, who knew Emma Irick, threatened to beat him up if he said any more. One thing was for sure: those who knew Rev. Emma Irick loved her deeply, and apparently one was even willing to fight for her.

This interesting pioneer was ordained by General Superintendent Phineas F. Bresee on September 11, 1911. The last paragraph of her autobiography, *The King's Daughter*, shows her optimistic view of service in ministry: "My happiest day was not when I was converted on October 23, 1902, nor when I was sanctified wholly on February 11, 1905, and not when God called me to preach. These were all great days in my life. . . . I recently celebrated my eighty-fifth birthday, and I am having the best time of my life. This is my payday."

Robbie Haygood Warren from the Lufkin, Texas, church, caught the essence of Irick's life when she wrote, "There were many lessons we learned from Sister Irick; for example, (1) never give up—God is still on the Throne, (2) 90 cents buys more than one dollar if you pay your tithes."

When Emma was five, her grandfather Wyland prayed on his deathbed that God would make her a blessing. Emma's first answer to her grandfather's prayer took place at age 8. When her mother was seriously ill, she went out under a peach tree in the orchard and asked God to save her mother's life to raise a younger sister, Eva. God answered her prayer, and she confidently told the family so. Her mother lived until Eva was 21.

Emma Wyland was born January 24, 1888, on a farm in north central Kansas. Since her mother was almost an invalid, Emma started cooking breakfast at age 7. She was keeping house when other girls her age were playing house. Emma began school at the tender age of 4, graduated from high school at age 16, and went immediately to Northwest Teachers College in Alva, Oklahoma. In her second year, she received a license to teach; her first school had 46 students in seven grades. She finished her degree at Alva in the summers.

Meanwhile, her family moved to Oklahoma and came under the influence of the Holiness people. When her father was sanctified, Emma said, "I need that too," so for three days and nights she fasted and prayed until the blessing came.

Emma's complete consecration to God included her call to preach, so the next logical step was Texas Holiness University at Peniel, Texas. There she came under the influence of E. P. Ellyson and "Uncle Bud" Robinson. It was also at Peniel, on November 16, 1907, that she received her first license to preach. That same evening she met her future husband, Rev. Allie Irick, who was already an effective evangelist, having just returned from a revival trip around the world with eminent, eccentric Greek scholar W. B. Godbey. Allie Irick evangelized for 35 years, holding an average of 20 revivals each year in the days when revivals lasted at least two weeks. He was the one who first called Emma "the King's daughter."

Allie and Emma were married June 16, 1908, just in time to attend the founding of the Church of the Nazarene at Pilot Point, Texas, on October 13, 1908. For years they were an evangelistic team, "Allie and Emma Irick," who traveled together, preaching on alternate nights. Rumor has it that listeners enjoyed her preaching more than his. Three children were born to them, and they were left in the care of others much of the time during school years. In the summer of 1931, Emma received a call to pastor the church in Lufkin, Texas. The building was in a bad state of disrepair with a roof that leaked badly. It was difficult to rally men and money to reroof the church, but it had to be done, so Emma climbed up on the roof to fix it herself. Some of the men got the idea and shamefacedly came to do the work for her.

Emma held a revival meeting at Southgate Church of the Nazarene in Colorado Springs when she was in her 80s. The pastor said that on Sunday morning she preached in a red silk suit and a red hat. In her message, "The Divine Advocate," she set the scene in a courtroom and had the Holy Spirit plead the case for us, the defendants.

Here is some of her testimony from her autobiography, *The King's Daughter:*

> There were many times as a teenager that I had fears of failing to live the sanctified life; but I soon learned to study the Word, pray habitually, and read all the literature I could find on the life of holiness. . . . Holiness will do more to help our present teenagers get their feet down and find themselves than anything I know. Personally, I never would have made it without the indwelling of the Holy Spirit.

—*Neil B. Wiseman*

A Mighty Mite Who Opened
Scripture to Thousands: Earl C. Wolf

His fellow students at Eastern Nazarene College dubbed him the "mighty mite" because of his small size. At 5'3" he did not remind anyone of a professional football linebacker. But by the time he graduated summa cum laude in 1939, the word "mighty" did not seem out of place. Even that did not necessarily predict the impact of Earl C. Wolf on his church and the people he served.

Born in Johnstown, Pennsylvania, in 1911, Earl was reared in a Christian home. His father, a worker in a steel mill, was 48 years old when he came back to God and accepted an earlier call to the ministry. That Christian home helped shape Earl's values and priorities.

During teen decision years, Nazarene evangelist George Woodward persuaded Earl to enroll at Eastern Nazarene College. His major work there was in philosophy and theology. Later he received more advanced training at Evangelical Reformed Seminary in Pennsylvania and also at Seattle Pacific University.

Earl Wolf married Mildred F. Nicholas in Pittsburgh shortly after he became pastor of the Church of the Nazarene at Stamford, Connecticut. Other pastorates were at Lancaster, Easton, Norristown, and Oxford, Pennsylvania. Three children were born into their family. His ministry beyond his local churches included service as NYPS (Nazarene Young People's Society) president, district Church Schools chairman, advisory board member, and trustee of Eastern Nazarene College.

Always a lover of humor, Earl often regaled his coworkers with stories of his time in the Dutch-speaking area near Lancaster, Pennsylvania. Some of the Dutch people use English words but in the old sentence form of their ancestors. Thus, a lady tired of neighborhood children might tell them to "go your own house over, sit your own porch on!" or "throw your own house over the ball!" He told of a Dutch pastor preaching from the text "The devil [goes about] as a roaring lion . . . seeking whom he may devour" (1 Pet. 5:8, KJV). The three points of his sermon were "(1) who the defil he is, (2) where the defil he goes, and (3) what the defil he is roaring about."

After 16 years in the pastorate with the added district and general responsibilities, Earl was invited to join the Department of Church Schools as adult editor. The move to Kansas City was a major one for him, since he had spent all his ministerial life in the East. His duties now became worldwide in scope. And going from the duties of the pastorate to that of writer, editor, and administrator was a challenge to this unassuming man.

The name of Earl C. Wolf appeared as editor of the adult materials in the Department of Church Schools from 1955 to 1972. His main task was preparing the *Adult Bible School Quarterly* (circulation 185,000 copies), and the monthly teacher's *Bible School Journal,* planned to aid 31,000 teachers of adult Bible classes. During that time, he also wrote 10 books of Christian guidance. Very few people ever have the opportunity to open the Scriptures to so many people so often.

In 1962 Earl was named director of adult work, adding administrative responsibilities to his editorial work. In that capacity he served as director of the Home Department and director of Christian Family Life from 1962 to 1972. At this time his alma mater, Eastern Nazarene College, conferred on him the doctor of divinity degree.

During all of his headquarters duties, he stayed close to the work of the local church. He preached in a least two revivals every year in local churches, "doing the work of an evangelist." During all those years, he also conducted workshops and other speaking assignments as a staff member in 225 church schools conventions across the United States and Canada.

Earl retired from his general church assignments in 1982. But retirement did not bring inactivity. He and Mildred moved to St. Louis to be near a daughter and her three children and began to serve in the Florissant, Missouri, church. Mildred served as director of the prayer chain for five years, and Earl taught the senior adult Bible class until he retired from it in February 2000.

A worthy life does not end when activities lessen. The influence of sermons preached, pastoral calls and prayers, organizational leadership, and Christian writing continue in the long shadow of a godly man's influence for the kingdom of God.

—*Albert F. Harper*

The Physician Who Was Always Available to Africans: Samuel Hynd

When Samuel Hynd's wife, Rosemarie, died in a tragic car accident in 1974, masses of Swazis attended her funeral. The king's counselor was there to give a word from the king. He said, "Ukossana Hynd was always available." The missionaries in attendance took note that the Swazi interpretation of "Christian" was "available." Rosemarie had spent much of her missionary activity among the king's village, mostly among his wives who had otherwise been neglected because they were polygamists.

"Available" also describes her doctor husband, Samuel. He had grown from babyhood in Swaziland, and the native people regarded him as one of them. He spoke their own language as fluently as if he were one of their children.

It's difficult for Americans to understand the complications that arose during Samuel's time of service. When his father, David Hynd, built Raleigh Fitkin Memorial Hospital, he obtained permission from the British administrator on behalf of the British Crown. Under the "protectorate" of the British, large sections of Africa were under one rule.

However, during Samuel's years of service, that protectorate was finally abolished, and the various tribal groups under different kings assumed complete control of their own territories. Thus, there was not the freedom of movement across the country that they had known before.

Allow me to share a personal experience to make that point. On my way from Mozambique to visit in Swaziland, I had to stop at a police station at Manzini. When I presented the note from my country and the note from Samuel Hynd, the police said, "Your signature means absolutely nothing to me, but the signature of Samuel Hynd means everything."

This incident also shows the exaggeration of the difficulties on the mission fields. Besides primitive conditions, lack of sanitation, ignorance, and superstition, there are the added hindrances of countless petty chiefs, satraps, and local customs.

This makes obvious the additional ability of Samuel Hynd,

as a native brought up in their own culture, to adapt to the new situations. As a medical doctor, he could speak to their physical needs; as a native, he could speak to their culture; and as a Christian, he was always *available* when they needed him. Spiritually, the Swazis thought of him as their own special Swazi son who became their special doctor.

Samuel Hynd was special to the Swazis because of his personal care for them. A glimpse of one of thousands of medical procedures shows his interest. On the operating table under a single bulb shaded by a green cover, Drs. Hynd and Kenneth Stark were doing a skin graft on a Swazi man's face that had been severely burned. They had taken a square piece of skin from his leg, cut it into tiny pieces, and were "planting" it like tufts of grass in a barren yard. The gentle, skillful hands of those surgeons mended many hundreds of Swazis.

The progression of Swaziland from a British protectorate to a nation kingdom gradually increased the problems for the hospital and other mission activities. The ministry there had grown from a hospital to a complex facility with grammar and high school facilities, a teacher training college, and a nurses' training institution. All costs became enormous as health needs increased and medical technology advanced. Outside resources diminished as African national leadership came into ascendancy. As a result, it became necessary for Nazarene mission leadership to turn the hospital over to the Swazi government. When that happened, Dr. Samuel and his wife, Phyllis, a nurse, opened a clinic that carries on the Hynd tradition of service above payment. The force of his own integrity has brought in necessary funds, enabling them to continue to provide health service at reduced cost.

In December 1998 Samuel was chosen by Queen Elizabeth II to receive the Commander of the British Empire Award. Samuel's father, David Hynd, had received the same honor from King George VI in 1944. The citation reads very simply, "For services of medical missionary work in Swaziland." Samuel declared, "It is also immeasurably shared by the Church of the Nazarene, which generously participated through nurses and doctors, prayer and financial support for more than fifty years."

Could it be that there are new "available" Nazarenes to serve millions yet unborn who will need the kind of loving care that these generations have received from the medical missionaries?

—*Floyd J. Perkins*

The Giggly Greeter at "Bertha's Door": Bertha Bruce

Could God use a lady with a silly little giggle and a crooked eye? Absolutely.

She was born Bertha B. Bruce in 1905 in Nashville. At age 8, she and her mother, who was stricken with typhoid fever, were cared for by Miss Blackburn, a teacher in J. O. McClurkan's Bible Training School. When Bertha's mother died, her father gave her to Miss Blackburn to raise. Under Miss Blackburn's tutelage, she was immediately led to the Lord in August 1913. She attended the Bible training school where her mentor and surrogate mother taught, and then Trevecca College. These schools were part of J. O. McClurkan's Pentecostal Mission before they became part of the Church of the Nazarene.

At Trevecca Bertha's classmates remember her spunky, humorous, loving ways. "She was always running around with a little giggle, helping others, and never had a bad word to say about anyone." She got her giggly, fun-loving nature from her heredity; her love and commitment to service came from her encounter with Christ as a girl of 8. She got her crooked eye from standing too close to where J. O. McClurkan's son, Emmett, was swinging a claw hammer.

The Nazarene Weekly, May 27, 1979, said of her, "Whatever she does is with a hop, skip, and a couple of jumps. But more than all, she has been a vital Christian example for generations to observe and pattern their lives. She is a rock in a weary land."

During the World War II years, Bertha made sure that all the members of the military from Nashville First Church of the

Nazarene received a constant supply of mail. And at the Sunday night youth meetings, she read their responses. She saved those letters for over 30 years, then gave them back to the former service personnel as a reminder of God's faithful care.

Another example of her concern for others was her organization of group trips to Billy Graham crusades. On one of them, more than 200 traveled to Los Angeles. Other trips included Portland, Oregon; Philadelphia; and Winnepeg. Along with this was her avid use of cameras to record the events. She had photographs of herself with Billy Graham, a governor of Tennessee, a postmaster, and even two Canadian Mounties.

After the need for keeping in touch with the servicemen ceased at the close of World War II, she became a church greeter. She stationed herself at one of the doors of the church to welcome any and all who came. She was more than just a greeter, however. She handed out the bulletins, patted the little ones on the head, shook hands, expressed concern for those going through trials, and on Easter Sunday had small Easter baskets made from strawberry crates. That entrance to the church was eventually officially named "The Bertha Door." Her ministry reminded all she touched of the scripture, "I would rather be a doorkeeper in the house of my God" (Ps. 84:10).

Little giggly Bertha had one outstanding weakness—she loved sweets. When faced with some tempting dessert she loved to say, "Get thee behind me, Satan—and push!"

Given that one weakness, her servant spirit knew no bounds. When Trevecca's president Willliam Greathouse was elected president of Nazarene Theological Seminary at Kansas City in 1968, Bertha did much of their packing and then went to Kansas City to help them unpack. Again, in 1976 when he was elected general superintendent, she provided the same service even though she was 71 at the time.

Bertha often laughed as she told friends,
"God didn't make me beautiful—
He didn't make me bright—
He didn't make me rich—
So I have to be sweet!"

It's true—Bertha has been a sweet servant of God possessed of many other saintly attributes, but she is still the little lady with the silly giggle and the crooked eye whom God chose to be a catalyst to encourage and effect changes in countless lives. Now, with her mind incapable of significant memory, with a little, high, shrill voice, she still repeats a timeless testimony, "I've lived a good life; God has been good!"

—Jo Ann Law

The Olsen Hustle and Holiness: Gordon Olsen

As I boarded the bus at the Mid-Continent Airport for downtown Kansas City, I spotted my friend Gordon Olsen. I was soon being treated to his typical testimonies of God's blessings, told in his rich, engaging voice, totally without embarrassment. Since I had been his pastor in the late 1940s, I was acquainted with much of the background, and I always loved his exuberant spirit.

One story, however, was new to me. He told how he and his wife, Rhoda, faced something shocking and totally unexpected—being hit with a $300,000 bill that was not theirs. When Gordon sold their refrigeration business, he had bigheartedly signed the papers to assure the new owners of entree to the banks. Now they had defaulted, and the bank was demanding the money from Gordon. It was either dig up or go bankrupt. The test was compounded by the fact that they had just pledged $1,800 a month on a new church building. At first they thought they would be justified in canceling; but after prayer, they resolved that they would make their monthly pledge payments as long as they had any money in the bank. God prospered them, and within three years the entire debt was paid—without missing a single monthly pledge payment.

This was typical Olsen style. Perhaps Gordon's upbringing figured into his character ruggedness. Born March 10, 1910, he grew up on a wheat ranch in southern Saskatchewan in a devout Norwegian home with three brothers. Not only did the boys learn to face hardships, but they also learned the power of prayer. At 4 years of age, Gordon was stricken with polio, which left him in a wheelchair, facing the doctor's verdict that he would never walk again. But his mother prayed otherwise. One day, she suddenly said to her son, "Get out of the chair and walk to me!" To the amazement of the family, he got up and walked to his mother—healed. While he had a slight limp the rest of his life, every other effect of the polio was gone, and he became a dynamo of energy.

At 14 years of age he made his way to Northwest Nazarene College in Nampa, Idaho, where he completed high school, then worked his way through college earning, in addition to his bachelor of arts degree, a master's degree in education. Along the way he found time to court a beautiful young woman, Rhoda Barbezat, the daughter of a Mennonite Holiness preacher. They were married in 1933.

Another life-shaping event was his clear-cut sanctification, experienced in a college chapel service. He later testified that when he was making his consecration, the devil painted a dark picture of the future; but "everything he told me was a lie." It was this experience that purified his motives and made his interests God-centered. It gave him courage to stand by his convictions even when it seemed costly to do so.

The force of Gordon's personality and unusual skills is reflected in the fact that his first job out of college was the superintendency of schools in Star, Idaho. After 5 years in that position, he became business manager of Boise (Idaho) Junior College. A stint of owning and managing a grocery store followed. Here he was threatened by irate customers with certain failure because he and his partner would not sell tobacco. But God honored them, and they not only made a living but later sold the business at a profit.

When World War II broke out, he soon found himself involved in the war effort in the shipyards of Portland, Oregon, as an efficiency expert. His job was to help workers find ways to accomplish more with less wasted motion. In Portland, just as in their previous locations, Gordon and Rhoda threw themselves wholeheartedly into the local Nazarene church. They became involved with Eastside Church, now Central Church. Only now there were four, for Gordon Jr. and Galen had joined the Olsen family.

After the war, Gordon decided he wanted to go into sales and applied for a sought-after position with a fast-growing firm. Out of many applicants, he was selected and one day found himself in the office of the president, who said to him, "Now we know you are a religious man and have certain personal scruples. But I need to remind you that you will be selling for us, and there may be times when you will be expected to arrange for activities that you personally may not approve of."

Gordon reported that as he sat there a moment, in his mind flashed the picture of his wife and two little boys and of the Nazarene church into which they had been pouring their lives. It didn't take long for him to make a strategic decision. He smiled, picked up his hat, and said, "I'm sorry—I think there's been some kind of mistake. Good-bye!"

So he and fellow church member Lester Quick moved their families to Eugene, Oregon, and went into the refrigeration business, where they built an organization that at its peak employed 80 people. After some years he sold out and focused on property and money management, acquiring in the process large real estate holdings and managing millions of dollars.

Gordon and Rhoda were never too busy to take on one more job in the church. For many years they managed the district camp meeting. Their giving of energy and time as well as money was legendary. When the younger son, Galen, was a seminarian in Kansas City, he once said to my wife, Amy, "When we were growing up, there was never any question as to which would come first, the church's interests or our own. It was always the church, and we never expected anything else."

In spite of heavy business responsibilities, Gordon was a phenomenally successful Sunday School superintendent wherever he lived. This was his first love. But in addition, he served on the District Advisory Board, the Board of Regents of Northwest Nazarene College, and for 25 years the General Board of the Church of the Nazarene. While God never called him to preach, to his personal disappointment as a young man, he became a popular inspirational speaker.

One Sunday in 1977, he arose early as usual. Rhoda turned over just enough to wave good-bye, and he, with his ubiquitous yellow pad, slipped out to a restaurant that he frequented to get ready for the day. Soon Rhoda was aroused the second time, but then with the news that while sitting at the counter, Gordon had quietly slumped over and gone to heaven.

Gordon's legacy is incalculable and ongoing. His was a rare talent, devoted with equally rare consistency to what matters most—an example, to be sure, of "holiness and hustle."

—*Richard S. Taylor*

Pastor's Wife Par Excellence: Emmelyne Miller Helsel

Emmelyne Miller Helsel is an inspiring spiritual example to all who know her. Even after the death of her husband in their retirement in Bethany, Oklahoma, you would find her totally involved in the local church activities. What a blessing to the pastor and staff.

After retirement, Emmelyne worked at the library of Southern Nazarene University for several years, enjoying the friendships she made there as well as at Bethany First Church, where she worshiped.

She also kept busy writing the children's stories for the WOW (Wisdom of the Word) Bible study program. To help with writing and keeping in touch with her family, she learned to use the computer during this more advanced time of her life.

What else was special about her?

• She married her love—a preacher—in the depression years, and they began their ministry "on the range" in Montana.

• She experienced the normal moves of pastors' families, going from one coast to the other and then back to the Midwest and finally to Bethany for retirement.

• She was an ideal parsonage queen for C. Kenneth Helsel

and a loving mother to two sons—Charles, who followed his father in the ministry, and Bob, whose career included law enforcement and education—and daughter, Laurel, who with her husband has been involved in Christian education.

• She has never displayed a negative attitude. Years after losing her husband, she spoke to the 100 people gathered in Bethany to honor the influence and memory of the Ford, Kansas, church, which closed in the 1960s. One of her comments was that she had nothing negative to report about her days in the parsonage. That's grace!

• She has a wonderful sense of humor including an outstanding ability to laugh at circumstances.

• One game of the family was to name the parsonages where they lived, from the "mission house" to the "cracker box" to the "cockroach motel." By the time the Helsels came to pastor at Ford, the church had been able to upgrade from the original parsonage to one large enough for the children plus a furnished guest room that was very special to Mrs. Helsel, who took such good care of it. The city of Ford is located midway between the east and west ends of the Kansas District. When the room was not occupied by an evangelist or the district superintendent, the Helsels were gracious hosts to others as well. Her record of guests, many to whom she served a meal, is long. The name given the Ford parsonage? The "halfway house."

Though coping with the health problems, Emmelyne Helsel continues to be a joy to family and friends. Her children encourage her to adopt the goal "Mother, think 100!"

If you don't ever meet the ideal pastor's wife here on earth, look for Emmelyne in heaven.

—*Colleen K. Cornwell*

V—O May It All My Powers Engage

A Church Leader from Walker Holler: A. L. Parrott

The young widow Parrott was on her way from Virginia to east Texas with her brood of boys in a covered wagon. Her brother had agreed to help her raise her boys if she could get them to his place. But the youngest boy had either chicken pox or measles, no one knew for sure. The wagon master issued this quarantine: "Maam—you can stay here with your boy, or you can leave him and come back after him. But in no case can you take him along! His pox will infect the whole train, and I cannot allow that."

With no other choice, she left the boy with a family named Thompson in Walker Holler, Kentucky. But she never returned. The boy grew up and married and had two sons. One of those two, Tom, also grew to manhood, married, and had two sons. One of them was named Alonzo.

Tom Parrott, Alonzo's father, lived in a log cabin near a spring at the bottom of Walker Holler. The boy's early school was on the rim of the snake-infested holler, and he rode a mule up the hill for classes.

The great change in his life occurred when he was converted in a "schoolhouse revival" in that same school building. It was a conversion so genuine that the evangelist sent him to Nashville to attend Trevecca Nazarene College on the Monday after the meeting closed. He arrived in Nashville with all his worldly goods in a valise and three dollars in his pocket. A. B. Mackey, president of the college, enjoyed saying that Alonzo Parrott was the only student to arrive at Trevecca with nothing in his pocket, and when he left, the college owed him.

After serving with pastoral effectiveness and dealing effectively with a financial crisis in the Clarksville, Tennessee, church, he was called to pastor Bethany, Oklahoma, First Church. The college next door was a fast-growing center of the Holiness Movement. Here he served as pastor, business manager of the college, and professor of economics. As pastor, he built a new church facility and parsonage. On a bright Sunday morning, he led the congregation in a march from in front of the old stone auditorium that C. B. Jernigan had built years before around the corner to the newly constructed building, singing "We're Marching to Zion."

As business manager, he led in a church-to-church fund-raising campaign that helped construct several major buildings. As pastor, he was interested in the community, being part of the campaign to build the first sewage treatment and water plant. When the Great Depression came on, he stood at the door of Farmer's State Bank in Bethany and assured the people that their money was safe. It was.

When Parrott was in his late 40s, he was elected president of Olivet Nazarene College, just south of Danville, Illinois, in the small community of Georgetown. The enrollment at that time was in the 200s. In November 1939 a disastrous fire destroyed one of the two main buildings. The college had endured several crises and nearly closed several times before. This looked like the end for sure.

But out of the ashes hope began to arise. The idea of moving was considered. Some thought of relocating to Indianapolis, while others favored Des Moines. However, with only one dissenting vote, the Board of Trustees voted to purchase a vacant campus in Bourbonnais, Illinois, near Kankakee, about 90 miles north of their old location and 50 miles south of Chicago.

In 1940, Dr. Parrott again began a church-by-church campaign to liquidate the debt on the new campus. In just four years, Olivet was debt-free for the first time in its history. The college grew into a university at that location and is now justly respected for its fine campus, its scholarly faculty, and its continuing influence for good among the youth of the Church of the Nazarene.

There are others who could have pastored Bethany First Church. There are others who might have kindled hope out of the ashes of old Olivet and brought it to its new location near Kankakee. Others could have carried on a campaign to lift the debt of Olivet completely.

But only God could see those possibilities in a boy from Walker Holler, redeem him from sin, and grow him into a man of spiritual influence and savvy. A. L. Parrott's influence will continue into the future for as long as Olivet Nazarene University endures.

—A. Leslie Parrott and Les Parrott

The Overcomer Who Became a Human Dynamo for God: Geneva Gough

Like the Oregon Trail that her parents were on when she was born, Geneva's life was filled with hardship, adventure, and disappointment. She crossed a desert of desertion when forsaken by the husband of her youthful years. She forded the swelling streams of poverty with four small boys to support alone. Though the trail she trod seemed impassable, she kept her eyes on Jesus and made it through to the shining mountains of faith.

Geneva was born April 10, 1898. Her parents interrupted their covered-wagon journey from Indiana to Oregon long enough for her to make her entrance into this world. By the time they reached North Dakota, her parents had been on the trail long enough and decided to make the little village of Velva their home.

Several years later, when the Methodist Sunday School teacher of teenagers invited her class to attend the Nazarene camp meeting in Sawyer, Geneva wanted to go. Though she was not yet old enough, when the teacher found she wanted to go along, she invited her also. Geneva was converted at the camp meeting that night and began a most unusual and rewarding Christian life.

Not long after her conversion, Geneva joined the little Nazarene congregation in Velva. There she heard about the life of holiness. She sought and received the second blessing of entire sanctification. From then on she faithfully followed the Lord.

Following graduation from high school, she married a young man from a Nazarene family. Four boys were born to this union.

Before the last of the boys was born, her husband deserted her to marry another woman. While it left her heartbroken and penniless, Geneva never lost her faith in a loving God who promised to provide her every need. And He did. Her boys would often hear her praying or singing the hymns of the church. They attended every service of the church—she would let nothing interfere.

Geneva was an avid reader and instilled in each of her children a love for reading. She loved poetry and essays. Her fine memory and gifted capacity for speaking put her in demand in the church and community to recite poems and give readings.

In 1934, she married again, and to this union were born three more children. Her new husband was a farmer, and the Great Depression of those years demanded disciplined living. Together they served the Lord by assisting others with needs.

Though her education had stopped at high school, she firmly encouraged higher education in a Nazarene college. All of her children except one received a degree from a Nazarene college. Three of her children have been ordained as Nazarene ministers, one was married to a Nazarene pastor, and one was a missionary in the Philippine Islands for 30 years. Two of her grandsons have been ordained as Nazarene ministers, and a granddaughter is serving as a missionary in Kiev. Her great-grandchildren are attending Nazarene universities.

And practical jokes. One time during camp meeting, she dressed up like a bum and went to the service. She sat near her friends, and they moved. Then she moved near someone else. Finally she acted as if she were taking money from the offering plate, and that did it. A brave usher escorted her out of the meeting. The "bum" disappeared, and Geneva came back in to listen to what her friends had to say about the incident.

After the death of her second husband, Geneva took a much more active interest in missions. She helped provide funds for a chapel at the Bible college in Baguio City, Philippines, and a residence for married students at the seminary in Manila. By careful management and shrewd investments, she could have lived in any style she chose. And that's what she did—she chose a simple, four-room house with one bathroom, giving the rest of her estate to the church and her children.

Geneva married again. Her husband, Rev. W. I. Gough, was a widower. They continued in the ministry for nearly 21 years until his death. Their final years were in Oregon—so Geneva finally made it to Oregon in 1972.

Geneva Gough's Oregon Trail, where she met and blessed many other pilgrims, was a shining pathway to the City of God.

—*Marly Anderson*

Gold Mine Evangelist in South Africa: Joseph Penn

In 1932 my father, Joseph Penn, was assigned to evangelize the workers in the gold mines near Johannesburg. The gold reef itself is about 60 miles long, believed to be the richest gold mining area in the world. The miners, all Black, slept in compounds—large rooms where the bunks were arranged around the circumference and the middle part left open for gathering and eating. Thousands of men came to work in the mines, where they usually stayed for months.

My father was gone nearly every night visiting, praying, and preaching in those compounds where the miners lived. As a result, many men believed in Christ and were instrumental in the salvation of many others when they returned to their homes. Thus, the gold mines that made so many people economically rich also provided a rich spiritual mine of evangelism where men were redeemed from sin. Then they took the gospel back to their families and villages, but long-term relationships were hard to establish and maintain.

Several years after my father was no longer active in full-time ministry, I returned to Africa for a visit. In Swaziland an elderly African gentleman who introduced himself as a retired pastor told me he had been converted years before when he was a young man working in the gold mines. He told how he returned from the mine one day to the compound to see a white man speaking to the mine workers. He said he was amazed to see this man fall on his knees in the dirt and begin to pray for the salvation of the workers. He said it made such an impact on him that it led to his later conversion. He wanted me to know that the man was my father and that down through the years, he had been forever grateful to God for my father's influence.

My father, Joseph Penn, was that missionary. He was born June 6, 1896, and died March 24, 1991. He stood about 5'8" and weighed 150 pounds. He and my mother were the first missionaries dispatched overseas after World War I and were first assigned to Swaziland. Three single missionaries—Minnie Martin, Eva Rixse, and Ora Lovelace—were with them. Before his assignment to the gold mines, Dad was active in visiting and encouraging the pastors and lay believers in the thatched-roof churches. Since there were no automobiles or trucks, travel was by mule or horseback. It was his practice to witness to every person he met on those trails.

In the dry seasons, travel was relatively pleasant because the streams were small and filled with clear water. But in the rainy seasons, the missionaries had to put themselves in the hands of God as they forded raging torrents and wide rivers. Years later, as I crossed some of these flooded streams on a bridge, I became convinced that only God's mercy had spared my father's life.

Later, when my father drove a car, look out. His driving was notorious among missionaries and native Christians. Whenever he drove his car into the garage after a trip, he would pause, raise his hat, and offer a prayer of thanks for God's protection. On one occasion, he returned with a car full of fellow missionaries from Johannesburg. As usual, he paused and raised his hat as he bowed his head to pray. Anna Lee Cox, a missionary in the backseat, asked, "What's he doing?" They quietly told her he was praying. She responded loud and clear, "Well, the way *he* drives, he *needs* to pray!"

Joseph Penn was a man of prayer and the Word. He spent many hours reading the Bible. On any topic of discussion, he would quote the Bible as the final answer to any question. As far back as I can remember, my father was the first to rise in the morning. On countless mornings, I found him on his knees, and heard him pray around the world.

The mines where the men worked were dangerous and the toil unremitting. As a result of their work, the mine owners amassed great fortunes from the sweat of the laborers. That's humanity's way.

But the missionary's way is different. Men who worked in those mines, redeemed by Christ, are treasures that last forever. That makes Joseph Penn, the gold mine evangelist, rich indeed with heavenly treasures.

—Dan H. Penn

A Basque from Spain Becomes a Key Layman at Moses Lake: Sebastian Etulain

Sebastian Etulain was a Basque by birth. As a nationality, we Basques puzzle ethnologists. From a mountainous region in the Pyrenees between Spain and France, our origins are unclear. Short and square in physique, disciplined in action, and unalterably opposed to any kind of outside regimentation, we have a favorite motto: "Neither slave nor tyrant." The basic faith of Basques is Roman Catholic. Fewer than 100,000 Basques reside in the United States.

At the age of 18 in 1920, my father followed his older brothers and emigrated to the United States. He arrived $500 in debt for his ship's passage and went to work as a sheepherder in the state of Washington. When he died in 1983 at the age of 81, he owned wheat land as well as several other businesses, all of them successful. As he lay in a deep coma just before death, his pastor prayed for him as "a friend of pastors." And he was.

The story of my unusual Nazarene father begins with his conversion. His older brother, Juan, was converted in a Pentecostal church. Sebastian at first angrily refused to listen to his brother's witness. Later, he relented and was genuinely saved. Once he became a believer, his life of faith mirrored his background. The word *indirra* is used to describe the work ethic of endurance and fortitude that is considered by the Basques to be the mark of an ideal man. This basic nature, when coupled with strong faith in Christ, produced a man of rocklike character and quiet devotion.

The next milestone was when he met and married Mary Gallard. Mother was of the Mennonite, or Brethren in Christ, church. The Mennonites have traditionally been strong supporters of holiness in personal life, and many of them have had happy ties to the Church of the Nazarene over many years. Finding no suitable church of either of their previous connections in Ritzville, Washington, they began attending a small Nazarene church there. Churchmanship now became as much a part of family life as Dad's work ethic. They sent their sons to Nazarene colleges and participated in district activities.

Father was private about his giving. When someone was taking an offering that involved lifting a hand as a pledge, he seldom made his pledge known. On one occasion, the Ellensburg church had built a mock-up of a proposed project and labeled different pieces with various dollar amounts. Each person was supposed to take a piece that represented how much he or she would give. During the service, Father gave no indication of what he would do. Later, when he thought everyone was gone, he picked up most of the pieces. But someone saw him and reported, "I think he just about paid for the building himself."

One of my brothers said of him: "Sometimes trying to get money out of Dad was like the slim pickings of a woodpecker working a marble quarry. Still, once he became convinced of the soundness of an idea, his finances followed his mind and heart. So having pitched his tent among the Nazarenes, Dad tithed and gave like a well-oiled machine."

Indeed, my father epitomized the cheerful giver. In addition to his regular tithing, he liked to fund local church and district projects. He also supported Father Flanagan's Home for Boys in Nebraska year after year and sent the children of several pastors to Nazarene colleges.

In this regard, I recall a lesson I learned from him. Not yet a teenager, I had earned my first wages helping a neighbor with his haying. When I brought home the $10 check, Dad told me in his heavily accented English, "Now, sonny boy, you owe the Lord $1 as your tithe." My mother carried on this tradition too. Her recently probated will revealed that she had donated the only house she and Dad had built to the Moses Lake, Washington, church for its parsonage.

For all his self-discipline and stern ways, my father was not without a strong sense of humor. He often supplied the parsonage family with meat and milk. Being a sheepherder by background, he liked to slip in a package of lamb for those beef lovers. Former pastor Neil Wiseman recalls that when Sebastian found out that yellow was not the pastor's favorite color, he pushed a proposal through the board to paint the parsonage yellow.

There was another time when his stern, efficient, all-out nature backfired on him. In an effort to make the parsonage lawn green and lush, he fertilized it with strong sheep fertilizer. What an amazingly beautiful, fast-growing lawn resulted. Then Dad thought it unfair to expect anyone else to do the mowing, so he mowed the parsonage lawn twice a week for the entire summer.

For almost a half a century, from the late 1930s to his death in 1983, my parents were loyal supporters of three different Nazarene congregations. In central Washington, the churches at Ritzville, Ellensburg, and Moses Lake were all part of his heart and his faith. His diligence in his extravagant stewardship and the regularity of his attendance were all part of his native culture and totally consistent with his love for God.

—*Dan Etulain*

———— ≍◆≍ ————

A 75-Year-Old New Convert Who Helped Energize a Church: Mary Quackenbush

This is a story about a classy mature woman who found peace and joy in Christ late in life. Her newfound joy propelled her into a life of astonishing service for her Lord in years when others enjoyed a relaxed retirement. It changed her lifestyle and made her a shining example of what the love of Christ can do when followed by deep gratefulness.

Mary Quackenbush of Pompano Beach, Florida, retired and widowed, was a lonely older person. She had enjoyed a *good* life. Born into a *good* home where heaven is attained by *good* works, she and her husband reared another *good* family doing *good* things. Their family was influenced by a pastor who was a *nice* man serving a church full of *nice* people in a *nice* town; they had very *nice* services, they all were *nicely* dressed and behaved in a *nice* manner, and the pastor preached on Sunday morning about how they ought to try to be *nicer*.

Mary's children grew up and established homes of their own. She and her husband retired to Pompano Beach and built a retirement home. After living in that home 14 years, her husband died, and she was no longer "special" to anyone. The Holy Spirit began to talk to her about going back to church. Church had long been regarded as unnecessary, since they had done plenty of good works and had nothing to fear. But where to go? She had seen a bus pick up children for Sunday School in her neighborhood. The name on the bus, "Church of the Nazarene," sounded like a cult, one she had never heard of.

Soon some neighbors of a Catholic background told her they were going to that Pompano Beach church and invited her to go with them. She accepted their invitation. When she entered the church, she felt she had found a home—a safe place too. The choir came in singing "Something good is going to happen to you." To a lonely person who felt empty inside, this was a wonderful place to be. She found friends there, and when Pastor Keith Wright called on her in her home, he introduced her to the true Friend. Wright reminded her that her good works would not get her to heaven and that "all have sinned, and come short of the glory of God" (Rom. 3:23, KJV). She repented of her sins and found salvation, personal peace and joy, people who cared for her, and a reason for living.

Mary said of the years following her conversion, "This was a very emotional time for me. I wanted to make up for the years I had ignored Jesus and thank Him for accepting me. I wanted to pass the good news on to others, so I prepared myself by constant Bible reading, church attendance, and Christian fellowship. I taught junior girls in Sunday School, led a Bible study in my home, and worked on an evangelism team. All this training helped me grow in understanding and strength. I was determined that when asked to testify or work for the Lord, I would always say yes."

Mary, who was 89 when she said this, continued: "I am now firmly rooted in the Bible and prayer. I love the Lord with all my heart, and my one desire is to be like Jesus. This has evolved through the teaching, preaching, counseling, encouragement, opportunities for service, and friendship of my brothers in Christ, my former pastors—Keith Wright and Neil Wiseman—and present pastor, Crawford Howe. I am grateful for the patient nurturing that has brought me from a state of lostness to knowing that I have eternal life in Jesus. *Thank You, Jesus, that I now have the peace and joy that a personal relationship with You brings.*"

Mary Quackenbush showed what one joyful, radiant person can do for the work of the Lord. Though retired, she flung herself wholeheartedly into becoming a living witness for her Lord. Her enthusiasm greatly impacted the church she attended. She is a good example of the fact that age is no barrier to serving Christ. She became a mature mother in the faith to the Pompano church family.

Mary's example extended to her financial support. She tithed regularly of her ample income and many times gave liberally to special projects.

Mary is now with the Lord, but her works follow her. She continued to report with joy to the very end the wondrous thing God had done for her.

—*Neil B. Wiseman*

The District Superintendent from Skid Row: Jarrette E. Aycock

In terms of human misery, Skid Row in Los Angeles in the 1920s was no different from skid rows in other cities even to this day. Then and now, the derelicts, alcoholics, and homeless are an embarrassing burden to their communities and recipients of compassion from people of faith. Then and now, mission shelters and halfway houses serve a stream of pitiful broken persons. The dedicated Christian workers who minister to down-and-out people are often bone weary and disillusioned, but they continue on, hoping to win another like Jarrette Aycock.

It was a typical homeless, hopeless young man who stumbled into the mission in Los Angeles in the 1920s. He later testified, "I was bound for hell and would never have known Jesus if it had not been for the mission workers." He was Jarrette E. Aycock, who became a Christian, then a preacher, then an evangelist, then a district superintendent in the Church of the Nazarene.

One of the mission workers was a lovely young lady named Dell Davis of Garden Grove, California. Jarrette was attracted to her, but she refused to have anything to do with him. Later, when he was first asked to preach in the mission, it was just after Dell had rejected him. What could a young, spurned fellow preach about in a situation like that? He once reported, "I searched and searched for a text and finally came up with the psalm that said, 'I will bless the LORD at *all* times, his praise shall continually be in my mouth' [Ps. 34:1, KJV, emphasis added]."

Happily, Dell finally did accept Jarrette, and the romance led to marriage. The two traveled for years as evangelists. They were always a sought-after team about whom another evangelist remarked, "It's no wonder Jarrette is so much in demand as an evangelist—he has the best song evangelist in the movement traveling with him all the time."

Jarrette had been an evangelist for 27 years when the Kansas City District Assembly was unsuccessful in electing a superintendent. The assembly voted to have General Superintendent R. T. Williams appoint one. Without hesitation, he arose and said, "There is an evangelist who has been running around the country for a long time, and I am appointing Jarrette E. Aycock as your superintendent." Aycock was there at the time and was as surprised as everyone else. He accepted the call.

As superintendent, Jarrette revealed the qualities of leadership that he had possessed all along. A genius at organization, a passion to not only organize new churches but strengthen the struggling ones, he led the district in growth. His attention to detail was legendary. In a zone rally at Lawrence, Kansas, C. B. Strang was the speaker. As I led the service, I told the people I knew our district would have great zone rallies with Dr. Strang because I knew the response of our people. I only had one worry, and that was how to finance the tour. Then I said, "But why worry when we have the best offering-taker in the business on the platform?" Then I turned to Dr. Aycock and asked, "Would you take the offering?" He always carried several humorous cards that he sometimes used to make a point. The next night at Independence, Kansas, he handed me a note written on the back of one of those cards: "Make same speech you did last night about offering and ask me to take it."

Just before he retired from the superintendency, Jarrette suffered a severe stroke but was determined to do the work of an evangelist, though his mobility was severely compromised. One young pastor remarked to an old preacher, "When Dr. Aycock retires, he will die within months, because he can't live without power, and his stroke has him so crippled." The older man replied: "You have it all wrong. He'll get in his wheelchair and hold revivals anywhere he can to keep telling about the miracle of grace he experienced in the Los Angeles mission." And that's what he did. He changed worlds from earth to heaven one night in a motel room just after having told the story of Jesus one last time in a revival service.

One of the great passions of Jarrette Aycock's life was to organize a mission in Kansas City for the down-and-outers like what he had once been. He talked it, promoted it, and took offerings for it until it became a reality. For him, this mission was an offering of true thanksgiving for the people who had helped him and a tribute to the Savior who provided an eternal home for one who was once homeless. That mission is still thriving today.

—*L. Wayne Sears*

God Transformed a Greek Tailor into a Hispanic Pastor: Julio Petridis

In 1921, in the same part of the world where the apostle Paul heard God's call, "Come over to Macedonia and help us" (Acts 16:9), a seven-year-old lad named Julio Petridis was orphaned in the fierce Greco-Persian War. Now he was fleeing for his life with the help of his older siblings. They listened each morning for the sound of gunfire and then went in the other direction.

At one time he even tried to walk a snow-covered mountain path in a pair of high-heeled women's shoes, because that was all he had. The boy's father was Greek, his mother Armenian. The fact that Persia separates Greece from Armenia emphasizes the striking contrasts and events that affected him all his life.

A refugee in that area of the world that today spawns and trains international terrorists was vulnerable to all the warring forces of that historical hotbed of hatred and cruelty. Hear the story of how that Greek lad, in the providence of God, became a leader of the Holiness Movement among the Hispanic population halfway around the world.

Having been separated as a teen from his other family members, Julio found himself in Constantinople, now Istanbul, where he worked as a waiter, masquerading for a time as an Armenian via forged papers until he was to be called into the Turkish army. Armenians were expected to help the Turks fight the war. To escape this fate, Julio boarded the first ship he could find and, without benefit of passport or visa, made his way to Cuba, hoping somehow to enter the United States. This was not possible, so he joined his brother in Mexico City, who had gone there several years later for the same reasons.

Upon his arrival in Mexico City, Julio knew only two Spanish words: those describing his craft as a needle and thread, *hilo y agula*. He was soon part of the large colony of Greeks and Armenians in the city. Then another of God's providences intervened. A magazine in the Greek language—somewhat like our *Holiness Today*—published in Syria by Armenians fell into his hands. He soon felt he should share with others what he had learned from it. He started a home Bible study. Reading carefully, he was able to see the way of salvation and gave his heart to the Lord. At the next Bible study, the group noticed something different about him. His Bible study was more effective and inspirational, and he immediately showed the Armenian-Greek group the way to salvation in Christ.

Now another almost unbelievable providential event happens. One day, quite by accident as the world counts accidents, Julio passed the First Church of the Nazarene. Wishing to grow spiritually and needing to learn the Spanish language, he began attending the church, pastored by Dr. Santin. He noticed the social hall and asked for permission to hold his Bible classes there. He also learned about the Nazarene seminary supported by our World Mission Division, where he could get help in learning how to become a pastor. When he enrolled, he did well in two ways: he learned to become a pastor, and he married the pastor's daughter.

Julio was ordained by James B. Chapman, who also asked him to plant a new church. But he was called to a church in southern California before they had the building completed. Beginning there, and during all his ministry, he was active in all aspects of the church and district. His influence is remembered by many young pastors who turned to him for mentoring. Whereas Paul sewed tents, tailor Julio sewed suits and with the money helped many both financially and spiritually.

As a mature Christian, Julio was a model for others. He loved peace above all else, which is not surprising considering his early experiences as a war refugee.

A final example of the contrasts in his life is that Julio spoke four languages: Greek, Turkish, English, and Spanish. Greek and Turkish to him early in life were the languages of war. In Spanish, he learned the language of love and holiness and skill as a pastor. Also, his wife was Hispanic. It's no wonder, then, that he always declared that Spanish is the language that will be spoken in heaven.

—*Pali Petridis with H. T. Reza*

Planter of Churches in Tough Places: Wilford C. McKay

God wants churches proclaiming the gospel wherever there are people. Wilford McKay accepted that challenge and served struggling churches most of his ministry. It was only natural, then, that to the people he served and his family, he was a godly hero of the gospel. He is an example of the kind of selfless devotion to Christ that has made the Church of the Nazarene strong. He gave without counting the cost. As a successful North Dakota farmer with a wife and small son in 1920, he felt God's call to the ministry. Like Abraham of the Old Testament, "He went out, not knowing whither he went" (Heb. 11:8, KJV). He sold his farm and livestock and moved to Pasadena, California, to attend Pasadena College to prepare himself for the Holiness ministry.

McKay worked as a carpenter to support his family while he attended college. On one job he was part of the crew who built the Rose Bowl; on another, he helped construct Bresee Avenue Church of the Nazarene. Later, these skills he used to support his family would be invaluable in building churches and parsonages.

Upon his graduation, the family moved back to the Northern Plains to begin a pastoral ministry that spanned nearly 45 years. The family's lifelong passion was missions. To overseas missions they gave financial sacrifice. To home missions they gave their lives.

McKay's craftsmanship in constructing buildings was complemented by his preaching. He shunned shallow emotionalism for strong biblical teaching. He believed the solid Rock was a better place to build than shifting sand.

Of the several churches he pastored in Idaho, Oregon, Montana, and North Dakota, the one in Nashua, Montana, serves as an example of vision, dedication, and sacrifice. In 1940 the district superintendent asked them to go to Nashua, a thriving church in a prosperous farming area. McKay looked the place over and agreed to go. But he also noticed that the next town of Glasgow, which was the county seat and larger, had no Church of the Nazarene. So he proposed that his family live in Glasgow, pastor the church in Nashua, and try to plant a work in the larger town as soon as possible. Since only 15 miles separated the two towns, the plan met with the approval of the district superintendent and the Nashua church.

Winding two-lane roads, blizzards and heavy winter snow, and five children in school all served to complicate the problems. He held morning and evening services in Nashua and Sunday afternoon and Thursday evening services in Glasgow. As children, we had good reason to wonder why we went to church all the time.

Then came World War II. Young men were drafted, building supply shortages were common, and all the laborers had gone to work in defense plants. All the efforts of the country were prioritized toward national defense. A wave of patriotism swept the country as a relief from the depression. Though it was a strong time economically, it had its drawbacks. People worked seven days a week, double time was paid, and everything was directed toward winning the war. There was also strict rationing of gasoline, and new vehicles were unavailable. Tires were often in extremely short supply. We drove on vulcanized retreads and prayed that they would hold together.

An air base came to Glasgow, increasing the population and the church. Meanwhile, Nashua was slowly ebbing away. The emphasis changed so that Glasgow was now larger and stronger than Nashua. We soon came to the point that we had to have a building of our own; rented halls were no longer suitable. With prayer and faith and determination, the building finally came to be—a monument to the vision, sacrifice, and tenacity of a man who honored God in all things.

Only eternity will tell the impact of the life of W. C. McKay on the world. His unassuming, unselfish commitment were an inspiration to many.

—L. M. McKay

Eccentric Evangelists Who Heralded the Good News: John and Bona Fleming

Many early Nazarene leaders were evangelists. They served as "town criers" of the Holiness message, bearing news of the new denomination from place to place. These men and women preachers carried the gospel seed from place to place, and became roving ambassadors who seemed to know everybody and everything in the fledgling Church of the Nazarene. Often their glowing reports of the last revival provided the spark of holy fire for their current campaign. In days of limited cross-country travel, they were the only seasoned travelers some people ever met.

The Church of the Nazarene owes the early evangelists a debt of gratitude because of the people they won who became key laypersons in many of our churches. Preachers and laity among the Nazarenes for most of this century could testify to being greatly influenced for good by an evangelist in a revival, youth camp, Holiness convention, or camp meeting.

Those early evangelists preached for instant decisions. Many were masterful orators who could move crowds. Truth was not tentative, and right was not relative. Destiny was uppermost in their minds. They hated sin but loved the sinner. Heaven was the goal of life and hell to be shunned at all costs. The coming of Christ was on the horizon. They honored the Holy Spirit. But this unanimity of purpose did not make them uniform—far from it.

As the organization of the denomination developed, revivals were the means for outreach, promotion, and growth. Often they were used to start churches. Two and sometimes three revivals a year were common in most churches. They sometimes lasted for two or three weeks—every night—and at the end of the series, they often received a large group of new members into the fellowship of the church.

Many of these early evangelists were eccentric, and some behaved like flamboyant religious entertainers. Others viewed themselves as prophets to call people back to God. Before radio or television, they often turned out to be the best show in town. And great crowds came to hear them. Some of them broke the highest attendance record of the local church during their revivals.

Brothers John and Bona Fleming were examples. They are chosen to represent evangelists not because they were typical in the sense of others being like them, but because their very individualism was typical. Both of them were transformed by the gospel, and it showed. Raymond Browning, himself an evangelist and poet, described John Fleming's conversion like this:

> *Bold and untamed as the swift moving panther*
> *Wayward and reckless, the talk of the town*
> *One night he chanced to attend a revival*
> *Heard Sister Hankes, and God struck him down.*

Being that kind of reckless, rash character, John's conversion produced a radical change in his life—so radical that he became as earnest in his salvation as he had been in his sin. His brother, Bona, soon followed him to Christ, and they began long years of evangelism as a team.

They were both bombastic in style. They wore black suits, white shirts, and celluloid collars. They were rather short and rotund in figure but had the presence of authority. They preached the Scriptures in their own eccentric interpretation. Their sermons were steeped in prayer, and they both emphasized a radical change in life in being born again. They stressed the demands of the Bible for holiness of heart and life.

Bona announced one night that the next night he was going to preach on a subject no one else had ever thought of. It turned out to be "My Little Toe." His text? "How beautiful upon the mountains are the feet of him that bringeth good tidings, that publisheth peace" (Isa. 52:7, KJV). No one reported the results, but you can be sure Fleming used the surprise element effectively. And the text was obviously stronger than the subject.

On one occasion John and Bona, out of curiosity, visited the grounds of a religious cult. When they began to ask pointed questions, they were told they were unwelcome there. One huge man with flowing beard and hair, who called himself the apostle Peter, started toward them in a ferocious manner. "What did I do?" Bona asked. "I ran. You'd run, too, if the apostle Peter got after you."

Bona believed in prayer and miracles. He loved to tell about a praying man in the high desert of California before the days of modern refrigeration equipment. His son became ill with a raging fever. The doctor told them that only if they packed the boy in ice would he survive. Ice in a desert? But the father and the church went to prayer. Soon a dark cloud arose. Thunder was heard and lightning was seen. "That's God's ice wagon," the man exclaimed. The storm came, it hailed, and the ice was available to save the boy's life.

A man came up to Bona after a service in which he used this as an illustration. "I enjoyed your sermon, Reverend," he said, "but I don't believe a word you said about that hailstorm."

"No?" Bona replied, in his high-pitched voice, "and you wouldn't have got no ice, neither."

—*L. Wayne Sears*

A Dance Instructor Who Became the Founder of a Holiness Mission: David Jackson Ford

God surprised us with another astonishing miracle of redeeming grace when He transformed David Jackson Ford, a dance teacher from St. Louis, into an effective witness for Christ.

Conviction seized the young man. He confessed his sins, gave his heart to the Lord, and like Paul on the Damascus road, answered God's call. The heavenly vision changed his life. That encounter with Jesus changed every part of his living. He set his heart on telling others about the Pearl of great price.

Hearing of the People's Mission Bible College in Colorado Springs, Ford went there and enrolled. Under the influence of the founder, a Holiness preacher named Lee, he developed a focus for ministry that turned primarily to the down and out. At the school he met and married another student, Florence Afflerbaugh. Upon graduation, the couple moved to Denver and founded the Denver Holiness Mission on Larimer Street, the "skid row" of the city at that time. They became members of Denver First Church of the Nazarene and established close contact with other Holiness churches. They held meetings in the mission six nights a week, along with a Sunday afternoon service.

Rev. and Mrs. Ford received help from many Holiness people, but their main source of revenue was the money he earned as

an employee at a glass factory. When asked why he took his wife
and their four daughters into mission work, he would respond
that God would watch over them. And he was right. The four
daughters—Mary, Bea, Ruth, and Esther—became exemplary
Christians, and all four of them married ministers. Mary became
the wife of Harold Volk, an outstanding evangelist. Bea married
L. S. Oliver, an effective pastor, district superintendent, and Bible
college president. Bea served two terms as president of the
Nazarene World Missionary Society.

Ford was always on the lookout for preachers. A barber was
cutting his hair and told him he felt a call to preach. Before Ford
left the barbershop, the barber was slated to preach at the mission.

Ford named Saturday night as Youth Night and soon had a
quartet of young preachers to hold revival services. One of them
was Wilbur Nelson, 17, who later blessed thousands with an inspiring radio ministry. Another was Earl Williams, 23, who became an influential pastor and evangelist. The third preacher was
Howard Hamlin, 16, who became a renowned surgeon, medical
missionary, and key lay leader among Nazarenes. The fourth
young man was Raymond Kratzer, 16, pastor and superintendent
of the Northwest District of the Church of the Nazarene.

Holiness people have always cared for the needy and outcast.
In fact, the largest social service organization in the world, The
Salvation Army, is a Holiness church.

Ford was an example of that kind of minister. His compassion showed itself in many ways. If an inebriated person came into a mission service he was conducting, he would go and put his
arms around the man to calm him so he could listen to the message. It is estimated that more than 12,000 souls found the Lord
as Savior during the 24 years that he operated the mission. That's
500 converts a year.

One could not be around Ford without feeling the presence
of the Lord. His kind, gentle spirit, along with his zeal for the
kingdom of God, moved people toward heaven's best. His fervor
helped people feel the reality of God. He believed heaven was a reality to be desired and hell a place to be shunned. Holiness of
heart and life were the passion of his ministry.

When he moved to his heavenly home, Ford could echo the

words of the apostle Paul in 2 Tim. 4:7: "I have fought a good fight, I have finished my course, I have kept the faith" (KJV).

—*Raymond Kratzer*

A Woman Whom Church Members Told Not to Preach: Delona McCraw Smith

On July 25, 1930, Delona McCraw Smith, 35, had just borne twin girls, three and four pounds each. She named them Ruth and Esther. Esther soon died, but Ruth survived, joining six brothers and sisters: John, Emily, Lester, Timothy, Joseph, and Samuel. It was that day that Delona settled her call to preach, an issue she had been considering for some time.

Soon after she said her final yes to God's call, district superintendent E. O. Chalfant came to console my parents on the loss of their baby. While there, he told Mother that he had gone to Westville, intending to close the church as a hopeless cause, but they had voted to call her to be their pastor. Her answer: "Tell them I'll be there in six weeks."

You can imagine the excitement in the small town of Olivet when the news spread that my mother—with seven children—had been called to preach. One day my father came home to tell Mother there was going to be a town meeting to tell her that she shouldn't preach, but he assured her that he would go with her. The day came, the people gathered, and after they had had their say, my mother rose to her feet and asked, "Which of you will stand in my place on the Day of Judgment and tell the Lord that you wouldn't let me preach?" The meeting broke up quickly and quietly.

Today, nine churches that she either started or helped revive stand in her honor. She pastored the church at Newport News, Virginia, her last church, for 27 years.

If you think that preaching was easy for her, you're mistaken. Just one part of the problem was the washing and ironing for a family of nine. Washing clothes back then meant a tub, a scrubboard, and an outside line for drying. It usually also included a black iron tub in the backyard with a fire under it to boil the clothes. My mother washed clothes one night and ironed them the next night so she could have time to call on her members and prospects during the day.

Starting a new church was also difficult. There were no home mission funds and no district assistance—only the quiet assurance that this is the Lord's will. She soon worked out a simple system for starting a church. She would go into a community, find a couple of ladies, start a home prayer meeting, then hold a revival and organize a church.

Take the case of the church at Yankee Branch, a community of several farm homes—a real population center. Mother went there and started a prayer meeting in the home of Mrs. James Collom, secured some land, and then announced that she planned to build a tabernacle in one day and hold services that night. She went back to Olivet, secured several students to help, convinced the power company to turn on the electricity, and by using a sod floor, she did hold services that night. Soon after that, she called the district superintendent to come and organize a church.

On one occasion, Mother heard that one of the children of a severe alcoholic was sick. She hastened to the house, and the man answered the door. She requested the privilege of having prayer with the child. The child was on a bed of leaves behind the stove, burning with fever. The child's father refused to call a doctor because "he would fuss me out for not taking better care of my family; no doctor can come here." Mother asked if she could take the child somewhere else and call a doctor, and the man agreed. She found a room, called a doctor, and saved the child's life. She went back a few days later, and the father gave his life to Christ and became a faithful member of the Yankee Branch church.

What price did her preaching have on the Smith family? Did she lose her children while she sought to save others? Not quite. Ruth, the baby who survived that night, and her husband are pastoring a Nazarene church now. Samuel pastored several churches, including Washington, D.C., First Church for many years. Timothy earned a doctorate degree at Harvard University. His dissertation was published under the title *Revivalism and Social Reform;* and, oh, yes—he also wrote the official history of the Church of the Nazarene—*Called unto Holiness.* Timothy also pastored the Wollaston, Massachusetts, Church of the Nazarene—the college church of Eastern Nazarene College—while serving as professor of history at Johns Hopkins University.

One reason for my mother's effectiveness was 100 percent obedience to God.

—*Ruth Smith Craig*

A Nobody Becomes a Somebody at a House Church: N. A.

A high-quality life started when N. A. was introduced to a tiny Sunday School in his Detroit neighborhood. The year was 1924. He was 12, and the Nazarene denomination was 16 years old. That association started a lifelong commitment to Christ so that the church became his North Star, his reference point, the center of his life.

Here's the inside story. Sophia Hoefler and Bessie Healey started a Sunday School in their homes on the east side of Detroit. The effort was directed mostly to their own children—plus a few neighborhood kids. The growing group forced them to move classes to their front porches, but that did not work well during Detroit winters.

Their strategy for growing their Sunday School was to visit homes, get acquainted with parents, invite children, teach Scripture, and count on God for the rest. Those were expansion days for the automobile factories, so Detroit experienced migrations of people from nearly everywhere, especially the deep South. So finding new children for their Sunday School was not too difficult.

Those two Sunday School women, Bessie and Sophia, followed up on absentees and rewarded faithful attendance by awarding Bibles for six months of perfect attendance. The women secured a promise of faithful attendance from N. A.

The growth of their Sunday School created a wonderful problem. Should they start a church? If so, what kind? How would they find a pastor? Who would support him or her?

Legend states that Bessie had a Canadian Nazarene relative who suggested the little Sunday School become a Nazarene church. However it happened, it became Detroit Second Church of the Nazarene. Their first building was a cement block house located in the middle of a residential area. That first property was secured in 1928, when N. A. was 16. Joyous singing, boisterous preaching, and frequent outbursts of shouting praises to God made the new little church the talk of the neighborhood.

N. A. became a charter member. Soon after the church was officially organized, the Ritter family trio came to sing in a revival meeting. They had a teenage daughter named Marguerite. The Ritters moved near the church building following the close of the revival. Within a few months, N. A. and Marguerite fell in love and later married, when he was 19 and she was 16.

For nearly 50 years, N. A. and Marguerite faithfully served God through this church, later renamed Grace Church of the Nazarene. Because of the usual shortage of personnel, they learned to do every job by simply doing it.

Across the years, N. A. and Marguerite attended district assemblies, camp meetings, and neighboring church revivals for spiritual refueling. Those events helped sustain them during lean times in the little house church.

Across those 50 years, the church moved several times from Dubay Street to a converted bank on VanDyke Street to a basement on Hoover Road. Finally, a beautiful sanctuary was constructed at the Hoover location. N. A. lived through all the toil and sacrifices until the church had a comfortable, permanent home.

Meanwhile, society changed and members moved to the suburbs. The question arose, Why not put two struggling churches together and sell Grace church? But the congregation refused to sell for money since this building was dedicated to Kingdom use. Though the building represented nearly a half-century of sacrifice, N. A. made the motion to donate the Grace property to the district for the establishment of an African-American church.

Fifty years on a church board and then leading an effort to give the building away was a gutsy, courageous, and even selfless act. When asked why he was willing to propose and support such a proposition, N. A. responded, "So they won't have to make the sacrifices we did for so many years."

The Nazarene called N. A. became significant in that little church. He invested energies—they paid off. He invested time—it paid off. He invested in friends—these friendships are still paying off to this day. He put the church in first place, and that gave him fulfillment.

I know the story well because N. A. is Neil A. Wiseman, my father. Without Dad's faithful service to Christ, I could never have become a pastor, a trainer of ministers, or a coauthor of this book.

—*Neil B. Wiseman*

A Florence Nightingale in River City: Ruth Lane

There was high drama at Olivet Nazarene College in the 1940s, 1950s, and 1960s. To people who live there, Kankakee, Illinois, is known as "River City" because the Kankakee River flows through it. The college had a new president, a new faculty, and some new buildings. But the real changes were in the student body. Serious-minded young men, veterans of World War II and many of them with families to support, joined in with the regular young people who are usually in college at that age.

The veterans were the major change—young men suddenly made old by the ravages of war—like Jay Pate, a lad from Arkansas who was sleeping below deck on the awful morning of December 7, 1941. Peaceful slumber suddenly turned into the nightmare of war: shrieking sirens, the thud of the first torpedoes hitting the ship below deck, the automatic doors closing so that many below deck could not escape. Jay led a few of his shipmates up through a small tunnel before it closed; their buddies never made it out. On deck they beheld a harbor full of burning oil and diving bombers. Jay lived to see another ship shot out from beneath him in the battle of the Coral Sea in the South Pacific.

Many of our students had suffered similar pain and difficulties of war. Bringing those war veterans home to the peaceful surroundings of a small Midwestern college and mixing them in with the usual freshmen created many interesting dynamics. "Drama" is not forceful enough to express those cataclysmic changes.

Those veterans were favored by the federal government with the G.I. Bill of Rights. But there were restrictions. They had to make passing grades in at least 12 semester hours, and if they worked a full-time job of 40 hours per week to support a family, it was a tremendous load. Only a few could hope to do that. They were caught in a bind between the demands of work and family, the course requirements, and the strict rules of the Veterans and Selective Service System. Then add the sometimes brutal winters in Illinois, and the medical needs would begin to increase greatly, exaggerated by long hours of work and loss of sleep.

Enter Ruth Lane, the school nurse. She took over Greer Medical Center, which consisted of two dorm rooms. A medical doctor came only one day per week. Ruth's pharmacy was stocked with mostly over-the-counter remedies, with no antibiotics. Every winter brought a serious round of sore throats, sinus infections, and flu.

With unusual cheerfulness, prayers, and long hours, Ruth cared for the more than 1,200 people who composed the Olivet family. She often returned to the office or dormitory after hours to see a patient or accompany someone to the hospital.

Students turned to Ruth to find solutions to many problems. She would sympathetically swab throats, give motherly advice, breathe a prayer, write an "excused absence" note, and send them on their way. She understood the trap they were in—things like excessive absences, extension of due dates, dropping a course, taking a low grade or an incomplete. She knew the power of humor, sympathy, and encouragement.

Ruth Lane was also a great churchwoman. She reveled in her Bible and hymnbook. She served on the church board and missionary society. Her patients saw her piety, and some knew of her own difficult personal struggles.

What will the tally show when the books are opened on Judgment Day? How many ministers and Christian workers would credit Ruth Lane with making it possible for them to continue to finish school? How many learned lifelong health lessons from her? How far and for whom did her prayers reach the throne? And when the student found a way to succeed and take up a redemptive life's work, did his or her accomplishments accrue in part to her credit?

When the problem seemed impossible, Ruth just went to prayer and tried a bit harder. She had a great measure of success. Everyone was better because of her thoughtful ministry to others in Jesus' name.

—*Willis E. Snowbarger*

The Air Traffic Controller Who Loves the Church: Odie Page

A commercial airline pilot once told me, "I always feel safer when my plane touches down at Charlotte, North Carolina, when I know Odie Page is in the control tower." Odie represents thousands of dependable Christian laypersons who serve the church with distinction.

Long ago the Church of the Nazarene decided we must have lay representation on almost every board and committee. Thus, you find faithful lay servants of the church on district boards, college boards, and denominational committees. Odie Page is an example of that kind of dependable leader.

Odie was born in Maury County, Tennessee, in the midst of the Great Depression in 1931. His father was a builder, but there was little building going on in those days. The life-changing event of conversion came to Odie when an evangelist held a brush-arbor meeting in their neighborhood. At the age of 10, one night Odie made his way to the altar and confessed his sins. Many times later he testified to his conversion in that revival.

After a time in Florida, the family moved back to Tennessee. Odie attended both high school and the college at Trevecca. It was there he met and married Ruby Geiger. As a college president I know said, "Marriages are made in heaven, but there's a branch office at Trevecca Nazarene College."

Odie served most of his working career as an air traffic controller at the Charlotte-Douglas International Airport. In the early years, small planes arrived in Charlotte from places like Columbia, South Carolina; Winston-Salem, North Carolina; and Raleigh, North Carolina. In Odie's closing days at the tower, big planes came from destinations like Frankfurt, London, and San Francisco. His work at the airport and his Christian journey have many parallels.

Odie and Ruby have been members of Charlotte Trinity Church for 45 years. He has been church treasurer for 43 years. They have been a loyal part of the growth and ministry of this church. Their daughter, Linda, now lives in San Diego, where her husband, Bob Brower, serves as president of Point Loma Nazarene University. Their son, Greg, is a member of College Church of the Nazarene in Nashville.

As his district superintendent, I often called upon Odie, a member of the District Advisory Board, to accompany me to a local church board meeting where a church was in crisis. Odie could talk to both the laypeople and the pastor as their friend. As a result, the emotions of the moment would often subside; and after a time of prayer, healing and ministry would begin.

The Pages were one of the couples who founded the North Carolina Lay Retreat. In a short time, more than 400 persons were attending this special event. The district assembly elected Odie a delegate to eight consecutive general assemblies. He served on the General Board of the church for 18 years as a layperson from the Southeastern Educational (Trevecca) Zone.

Odie has a wonderful gift for serving in places of honor without losing the common touch. The Pages always welcome lonely, hurting people into their lives and home. If the church is in a building program, the Pages are among the first to be involved in labor and financial support. On Sundays, Odie is usually teaching a Sunday School class. In revivals, he and Ruby are always there. They are examples of the Christian Holiness lifestyle.

—D. Eugene Simpson

VI—*Arm Me with Jealous Care*

The Woman Who Started a University: Mary Nesbitt

Without a sense of destiny, Mary Nesbitt, a young school-teacher, gathered a few children in 1907 to start a school at Georgetown, Illinois. Their classroom was a small frame building that her brother and others had constructed for a Holiness church. Almost no supplies were available. With few books and no blackboards, children sat in church benches intended for adults. When they wrote their lessons, the children knelt on the floor and used their seats for desks.

There were 36 children in the first class. During the first semester Mary's brother, Orla Nesbitt, and two brothers, Ed and Will Richards, built a small school building next to the church facility, and the enrollment increased.

The idea for a school came from a sermon preached by E. F. Walker, who later became a Nazarene general superintendent. He was an erudite former Presbyterian preacher who, after receiving the blessing of entire sanctification, joined the Church of the Nazarene. Walker's sermon on Christian education preached at the Eastern Illinois Holiness Camp Meeting near Georgetown became a life-changing event for Orla Nesbitt.

Over the next three years, Nesbitt and the Richards brothers bought farmland south of Georgetown on Illinois State Highway 1 and laid plans for a commodious campus with a grade school, high school, and college. It was to be a credit to both education and devout Christian living.

As yet, their ambitious beginning had no name. In a prayer meeting on the Nesbitt farm, a man whose name has long since been forgotten jumped to his feet and declared, "This place is going to be called Olivet!" That is the Mount from which Jesus ascended to heaven after telling His disciples to "go into all the world and preach the good news" (Mark 16:15). Such a local global view can be observed in many events and personalities in Nazarene history.

In the fall of 1908, after only one year, Mary Nesbitt's three-room school had moved to a new location, and Fred Mesche had been engaged to open the high school. Just before that, in June, the first camp meeting was held at the new location. On the last Saturday of the camp meeting, a group of seven men met on the Nesbitt farm and constituted themselves as a board of trustees. They elected L. Milton Williams as their chairman and A. M. Hills as the first president of Olivet College. Both had been speakers in the camp meeting.

Since there was a seam of coal underneath the ground surface and room for a corn crop, the salary of the first president included any income derived from coal and corn. That was a mistake. Hills was neither a farmer nor a coal miner.

Next on the agenda was the erection of their first major building, named Canaan Hall. They also applied for and received a charter from the State of Illinois as Illinois Holiness University in 1909. A theology department was added in 1911.

Many years later, in 1939, a disastrous fire destroyed the main campus building, and President A. L. Parrott led a move from the original campus to Bourbonnais, Illinois. The wisdom of that move is evident in the beautiful campus that stands there today. Fifty miles south of Chicago, with the support of the Bourbonnais-Kankakee area, it has taken its place as an outstanding university with a well-deserved reputation for excellence of education, purpose, and results.

Who would have imagined that Mary Nesbitt's small school in a makeshift church building, with few books, no desks, no library, and no chalkboards, could become a great university? It is a tribute to the vision and courage of those who started it and those who have followed and brought it to fruition.

All Nazarene colleges and universities share similar origins of faith, sacrifice, and devotion to Christ and His kingdom on earth. Nazarenes have shared the concern for the knowledge that comes from God and reaches for Him, who is Truth. These institutions of higher learning are still the cutting edge of the Holiness Movement. And the colleges and universities are testimonies to the sacrificial faith of those ordinary people who prayed and gave to make them come to pass.

—*Leslie Parrott*

The College President from the Tennessee Hills: Archie K. Bracken

Holiness revivals have often had surprising, eternal impact on the destinies of individuals. Archie Kay Bracken, from the hill country of western Tennessee, is an outstanding example. Though his beginnings were steeped in poverty, he grew to become a competent example of education with a devotion to Christ that many early Nazarenes possessed. He was a wholehearted Christian, a polished gentleman, a careful scholar, and a brother to every student who wanted to learn.

Bracken was ably supported in these commitments by his wife, Mattie Green Bracken. Together they raised a family of concerned Christians—their students. Though they had no biological children, their house was always home to young people who needed help. Of the thousands of students touched by Archie, his wife, and the faculty members of those days, many went on to places of leadership and service in the church as well as many other areas of society.

In Archie's boyhood, public schools in western Tennessee were almost nonexistent. Much of the problem stemmed from the residual economic hardships of the Civil War. These realities made education sporadic and limited for those who did not have the means to attend a private school. Bracken said of himself, "I was like the country boy who had trouble with the difference between printing and script writing. 'I can read readin', but I can't read writin'.'" His training was so meager that at the age of 18, he gave up, married a sickly young girl, and settled for a drab existence. When his young wife and the young son she bore died, he stood brokenheartedly at their graves and wondered about the meaning of his life.

Then came a Holiness revival. Remember—this was a time of lukewarm religion. Archie's family were subscribers to the view that "Christians must expect an up and down life. There were not many signs of triumph and victory. Salvation to Heaven in the end was affirmed but not real salvation from sin in the here-and-now. . . . I wanted to know the joy of Christian living. 'The Revival' brought this message of joy, victory and salvation from sin" ("Memoirs of A. K. Bracken" [Bethany, Okla.: Bethany Historical Society and Museum, 1976], 23). Archie gave his life wholeheartedly to Jesus Christ and went on to experience the joy and victory of entire sanctification.

Though his parents were not well educated, they had stressed to their children the importance of a good education. A sister paid him a dollar to read all the works of Shakespeare. He became a true seeker after learning, going from college to college as opportunity afforded. He married Mattie Green, who, like he, sought and obtained advanced degrees and made enviable records doing it. As a result, Archie taught in several schools where he was acting president before being called to Bethany, Oklahoma, in 1920.

Once each year he preached a memorable chapel sermon titled "The Banquet of Consequences." The sermon always began with these words: "Sooner or later each person sits down to a banquet of consequences for his own actions and failures." His text was Prov. 1:31: "Therefore shall they eat of the fruit of their own way, and be filled with their own devices" (KJV). Personal accountability was one of his most compelling convictions.

A. K. Bracken's foundational belief about education was that it is not for personal advancement of money, position, or prestige, but rather for self-development so that one may better serve Christ. "There is nothing better for chapel than good preaching, but a chapel talk is beamed more to personality development on the practical level. It should aim toward the level of practical Christian living and toward good citizenship, not only of the kingdom of God, but good citizenship of the home, the church, the school, ones job and of the state" (ibid., 30). Therefore, Bracken maintained, a Christian college is a place of preparation for dedicated Christians who will become soldiers of the cross of Jesus, who will live for Christ and others. They come for training; they go out to serve. They're not all destined to become preachers or missionaries, but they're all to be totally dedicated to Christ in their field.

Therefore, when commencement came, Bracken expected the graduates to go as soldiers into a lifelong combat with sin. The senior class would rise for the recessional, and at my graduation, Alline McGraw Swann with her dramatic touch on the piano played the march. We heard again the summation of President Bracken's dream for us all:

> *Lead on, O King Eternal.*
> *The day of march has come.*
> *Henceforth in fields of conquest*
> *Thy tents shall be our home*
> *Thro' days of preparation*
> *Thy grace has made us strong;*
> *And now, O King Eternal,*
> *We lift our battle song.*

—L. Wayne Sears

She Sacrificed Her Treasured Wedding Ring for Missions: Lucy Belcher

Hatley and Lucy were lifelong sweethearts, married for 60 years. And every day for 60 years, she cherished the ring he gave her on the special occasion of their wedding.

Hatley and Lucy were longtime members of First Church of the Nazarene in Clovis, New Mexico. For years they lived directly across the street from the church. As part of their devotion to Christ, they served as custodians, keeping the building neat and clean. Their usual habit was to clean the church on Thursdays, but one week Hatley decided to clean the church on Tuesday. Then suddenly he died, with the church already cleaned for his funeral on Friday.

After Hatley's death, Lucy continued her commitment to Christ and the church. She led a senior adult prayer group that met in her home every Tuesday. After the church moved to a beautiful new location on the other side of town, she continued her interest, prayer, and sacrificial giving. She was a true warrior who prayed for the pastors, the music, the Sunday School, and especially the missionaries. These intercessory prayer times continued long after her declining health made it impossible for her to attend services.

The Easter Offering for missions was coming up one year. At the staff meeting that week, Senior Pastor Gerald Wood brought a letter from Lucy. To the staff he read her letter, which included her golden wedding band that she had worn for 60 years—a truly cherished possession. The memories associated with it had brightened her life for many years since her husband had been suddenly called home. Tears flowed from the eyes of the pastor staff when she indicated her wish that the ring be sold and the money used for missions.

Pastor Wood said something must be done. The staff agreed. Then the suggestion was made that the letter and its sacrificial spirit be shared with the church at the Sunday evening service. Then contributions would be accepted in the offering, and the ring be returned to her. That night the congregation enthusiastically placed $300 in the offering for that purpose.

At the next staff meeting I, as senior adult pastor, was given the privilege of returning the ring to her. When I went to Mrs. Belcher's home bearing the ring, she warmly greeted me.

When I told her that I had come to report on her ring, she was eager to hear how much it had brought for missions. I asked, "Mrs. Belcher, would you believe your ring brought $100?" She responded, "Oh, I had no idea it would bring that much."

"Would you believe $200?" The tears welled up as she shook her head in wonderment.

"Would you believe $300?" The handkerchief in her apron pocket was needed by then. "Yes, Lucy, your ring was redeemed for $300."

"Redeemed?" she asked.

I brought the ring from my pocket. "Yes, Lucy, we didn't sell your ring, but your friends at church gave an extra $300 to their own Easter offering. Now I have the privilege of placing your ring back on your finger." Her hand trembled with joy as I placed the ring back back where it belonged, where Hatley had placed it so long ago.

Spiritual influence in a church? Building the Kingdom? Setting an example of joyful giving even of cherished possessions? Lucy Belcher was blessed, the cause of missions—the purpose of Christ's coming—was blessed, the pastor was blessed, and the congregation was blessed.

Lucy's offering of her wedding ring naturally brings this story to mind:

> Then Mary took about a pint of pure nard, an expensive perfume; she poured it on Jesus' feet and wiped his feet with her hair. And the house was filled with the fragrance of the perfume (John 12:3).

—Ray J. Hawkins

Jimmy Knew How to Shape Boys for God: James Pate

Every blade of grass was worn down in the backyard of Jimmy's home. We kept the grass tramped down playing basketball. His Sunday School boys were more important than a nice lawn.

Not that we were his only concern. James Pate also found time to serve as treasurer for the Tennessee District, trustee for Trevecca Nazarene College, president of the local youth group, and in many other assignments. Nashville First Church of the Nazarene was his life. He was the kind of layperson who makes a pastor's heart leap for joy. Regardless his various titles or many involvements, Jimmy's heart was full of loving concern for young men who needed Jesus. He made it clear to us that his first calling and deepest commitment was to do whatever it took to lead us to Christ.

I'm not sure where people like Jimmy Pate get their energy. I think it must be that when God finds an open channel like that, He pours everything needful through it into the task at hand. Jimmy had strength and energy for a group of rowdy adolescents as well as the more "serious" aspects of the church.

This God-furnished energy gave him the courage to tackle a class of boys. In 1943 he became teacher of the Victory Class—boys 14 to 17. That age spread in itself is an incredible challenge. He became a model for teaching teenagers. Sports was a consuming interest for us, so in 1947 he had the courage to organize us into a softball team registered to play in the city softball league.

In those days there was some concern over the spiritual value of softball, so we played as the Victory Class without the name of the church. Jimmy's love for his "boys" gave him the courage to risk criticism from others who did not share his adventurous spirit.

Since there were no church funds for uniforms, bats, balls, or other equipment, my father, Virgil Williams, was able to get some old uniforms from his employer, the Standard Candy Company. The product lines of the company were stitched into the fabric, so we had some rather interesting names as players. Names like "King Leo," "Goo Goo," and "Dream Cream." But Jimmy invested the time and energy necessary, and we became a winning team. Do you suppose the fact that we won the city championship that year had anything to do with our being allowed to use the church name the next year?

But even when we used the name of the church, we were still the Victory Class. You see, more than his interest in a winning softball team was his interest in spiritual victories. And those real victories came. I still remember the Saturday afternoon when practice was halted while one of our players watered the dandelions in left field with tears of repentance. Jimmy's love and prayers had broken through.

You know by now that in those days the church did not have multiple staffs with highly trained youth ministers. But we did have dedicated laypersons who, with the help of the Holy Spirit, a life dedicated to God, and a love for youth that leaped beyond all barriers, picked up the ministry and embraced the opportunity with enthusiasm. And they reaped the rewards of faithfulness to God.

Jimmy Pate went to heaven in 1975 at the relatively young age of 68 years, but he had lived a full life. Scores of us who were privileged to have him in our lives will join him on the playing fields of heaven one of these days. And somehow I believe that if there's an empty field tucked away somewhere in the corners of Gloryland, Jimmy will get enough help from the groundskeepers up there and find the equipment necessary to play a real "homecoming day" game with us. And there won't be a blade of grass on that field.

—*Gene Williams*

The Church Treasurer Who Never Knew How Much Is Too Much: George Goodwin

This is the story of a woman who prayed too much, a man who gave too much, and a pastor who sacrificed too much by the standards of the world. But it took "too much" to establish a church in "rock-ribbed" New England.

It happened in Norwood, Massachusetts, during wartime, when the effects of the Great Depression were still a part of everyone's life. Some people in Norwood opposed the Evangelical Holiness message. Wartime, when everyone was working long hours and Sundays, would make anyone hesitate to think of starting a new church. The depression had taught many to "make all you can, and hold on to it."

But it happened, not simply by human initiative, but under God's guidance.

District Superintendent John N. Nielson, whose three sons—Robert, John, and Joseph—made memorable records themselves, secured the use of a small, empty church building. He bribed a young man ready to graduate from Eastern Nazarene College to go with his wife to this place. He promised them $10 per week; he preached in the first service and then turned it over to us. I was that beginner pastor.

Like many others in those years, my wife and I went to work

to see what God would do. Our good friend Donald Brickley agreed to help for the first year. Calling, holding services, and praying, we began the work.

At first we were encouraged and then realized that a group of infiltrators who had practically emptied the church were of the "tongues" persuasion. Paul warned Timothy about this: "The goal of this command is love, which comes from a pure heart and a good conscience and a sincere faith. Some have wandered away from these and turned to meaningless talk" (1 Tim. 1:5-6). The intense fire of Holiness preaching soon solved that problem, and they moved to another church.

The next thing to do is have revival services. In wartime? When people are all working overtime? How are you going to pay for it? That's just too much! But then, "too much" is what it takes to develop a strong church. So we called another pastor, Arnold Woodcock. He and his wife, expecting their first child, came and shared the one-bedroom apartment while they held revival services. We all prayed and sang, and Arnold preached.

A pastor should be an example to his flock, so I went early the first night to be there to greet the people. But I was not the first one there. A lady, Mrs. Oen, was in the back pew praying silently. Those "rock-ribbed" Norwegians can surprise you too. The next night I went even earlier, and there again sat Mrs. Oen praying. Another night I was a half hour early, and once more there was Mrs. Oen praying. By that time I felt I needed an explanation from this lady, a hardworking Norwegian well past middle age. She told me that for many years she had made her preparation for revival as such: she would leave work early and fast her evening meal. Instead of eating, she would go to the church sanctuary and quietly pray until service time.

God honored our prayers. On the last Sunday night we saw the results for which we prayed. Several readily came forward to pray about their spiritual needs. George Goodwin was sanctified wholly that night. He came from a prestigious church that did not preach the gospel. He was concerned that his two sons and daughter find and follow the Christian way. We were finally able to organize the church, and George joined our little struggling group. In addition to teaching the adult Bible class, he served as treasurer.

That is when he did "too much." After several months, when I knew that the expenses were surpassing the income and the treasury always showed a positive balance, I asked George about it. He confessed that he had been adding to the balance on the side but did not want others to know it. During the war, when he had to work on Sundays, he quietly gave his Sunday wages in addition to his tithe and other offerings. When asked why, he answered, "Pastor, I need this church here in Norwood for my family." God honored his faith. All three of his children attended Eastern Nazarene College and excelled there.

Pastor Donald Brickley, Arnold Woodcock, and especially George Goodwin all learned by experience the truth of these words by Kittie L. Suffield:

> *Does the place you're called to labor*
> *Seem so small and little-known?*
> *It is great, if God is in it,*
> *And He'll not forget His own.*

> —Dick Howard

"The Good Old Days Are Now": Fred Ferguson

As I look back upon 56 years of service as a pastor in the Church of the Nazarene, I have happy memories of laypersons who made my ministry such a joyous journey.

As my memories travel back across the years, many names come to mind. However, one person especially stands out. When I became pastor of the church in Carthage, Missouri, a man named Fred Ferguson had retired from a career in business and had begun a new career as a helper around his home and was a good neighbor to many folks who needed assistance.

In 1948 I moved into the parsonage, which was just around the corner from the church. One of the first persons to greet me and my family members was this unassuming, gentle man, who came by to see if there was any help he could offer to the new parsonage family.

Brother Ferguson had a son who was the pastor of the Church of the Nazarene in Fort Scott, Kansas. He prayed daily for him and made it a weekly habit to come to the church sanctuary on Monday morning to pray for the work of his minister son and other members of his family. Often when he saw my car outside the church office, he would tap on my door and ask if I could join him at the altar as he prayed for his family members and for God to use me in my pastoral ministry.

I'll never forget one Wednesday night prayer meeting when we were hearing testimonies. Brother Ferguson stood to his feet, clapped his palms together, and shouted, "Praise God—the good old days are now!" The congregation was awakened spiritually as this excited saint expressed such contagious optimism.

Brother Ferguson faithfully attended every service of our 10-day revivals. He listened carefully to the evangelists' messages. When seekers came to the altar, he was always available to pray with them to realize spiritual victory.

His sweet wife quietly stood by him with love, care, and concern. I don't remember either of them ever exhibiting a critical attitude. To be in their presence was to sense a deep love and concern for all their friends and neighbors.

Brother Ferguson had many friends who were members of other churches in our city. Though not highly educated, he had the reputation of a good man. When I recall his life, I think of 2 Cor. 11:3, which speaks of "the simplicity that is in Christ" (KJV). Fred Ferguson's love for God and his neighbor was spelled out in a life that reflected the love of his Lord.

What a joy it was to preach to him! He never took his eyes off the preacher. His "Amens" were not loud, but his nodding head and warm smile were an incentive to the speaker to do his or her best to present the gospel of Christ as the hope of joy in this life and eternal life in a glorious future.

How thankful I am that God allowed my life to intersect with the life of a man who put his hand into the hand of God and sought to walk worthy of the One who had called and led him! It is people like Fred Ferguson who have influenced the Church of the Nazarene to be a force for God and holiness in every generation since the beginning.

—*Ross W. Hayslip*

Her Price Is Far Above Rubies: Mary Paxton Jerome

The Book of Proverbs describes a woman whose worth is far above that of rubies. Mary Paxton Jerome deserves that accolade.

Mary was born July 12, 1878. Her father was the Union gunner who shot down the last Confederate gun on the Mississippi River at Port Hudson, so Abraham Lincoln could declare, "The river is now free for passage all the way to the Gulf." She was a distant cousin of Jenny Jerome of Boston, the mother of Winston Churchill.

Mary and Wade were married on Christmas Day 1898 in the Methodist parsonage at Ingalls, Oklahoma, which was then Indian Territory. Soon after that, they moved to southwest Oklahoma and became involved in the Holiness Movement. In 1919 they moved to Bethany to be near Oklahoma Holiness University for their growing family. James B. Chapman was the pastor then, and he baptized their infant son.

When the Great Depression came, life changed greatly. During those years, Mary and Wade separated. Their children were on their own, and their finances were almost nonexistent. About that time, Mary, who needed a job, was offered the ministry of serving as a substitute mother to young women away from home. Rev. and Mrs. John F. Roberts asked her to become a part of the staff at the home for unwed mothers in Pilot Point, Texas. Though "Rest Cottage" was not an official ministry of the denomination, it was supported mostly by special offerings from compassionate Nazarene congregations. J. P. Roberts had started the ministry, and after his death his younger brother, John F. Roberts, and his wife, Grace, became the superintendents. In those days a strong social stigma was attached to unwed mothers. Nonetheless, Holiness people looked for ways to care for those who needed help. It was said that if a pastor called about placing a needy girl there, John F. Roberts would ask, "Is she a good girl?"

At Rest Cottage, Mary endeared herself to the girls and the staff members. They found in her a true mother with love, understanding, and a determination to allow the God of all grace to restore them to the paths of virtue and obedience to the best that was in them.

After several years there in Rest Cottage, Bethany Nazarene College needed her to serve as a dorm mother. College President S. T. Ludwig called Rev. Roberts, requesting permission to talk to her. The following day, Dr. and Mrs. Ludwig drove to Pilot Point, and that evening Mary was installed as matron in Bud Robinson Hall at Bethany Nazarene College, now Southern Nazarene University.

Discipline in a dormitory can be a difficult issue. The young coeds there are eager for life and new experiences, and they desire to be accepted into their new world. Such an environment always requires an understanding, fair leader.

Though some college girls had problems, they never seemed to be a serious problem to Mary. Her own life of discipline kept her calm and loving at all times. One of her former dorm residents, now a mature woman, recently told me, "When the girls on the third floor began to get noisy, Mary just calmly walked up there. They could hear her steps, and by the time she arrived, all was peace and quiet."

Her self-discipline led her in her prayer life. Her own children at home knew that she had a period of prayer every day. When that time came, she retired to her closet, and they could hear her "private" devotions sometimes all through the house. Her neighbors knew not to call at that time of day.

Mary's self-discipline led her in her Bible study. For years she read her Bible through every year. Her children and her "dorm girls" were the recipients of her knowledge of the psalms, the heroes of the Old Testament, and the words of her Lord. She could quote many passages from memory.

Mary's self-discipline and knowledge of the Bible made her a discriminating listener. She remarked one time that when James B. Chapman finished with a portion of Scripture, he had "said everything that needed to be said, and nothing that did not need to be said about that subject."

Mary was my mother. Soon after she resigned at Bethany, she and Wade were reconciled, and I had the privilege of performing their remarriage ceremony. She continued her life of intercession to the end. At the age of 87, while out Sunday School calling, she fell and broke her hip. She went to heaven soon after that.

As with so many other Nazarene mothers of influence, both natural and adopted, it could be said of my own mother, "Many daughters have done virtuously, but thou excellest them all" (Prov. 31:29, KJV).

—*L. Wayne Sears*

VII—*Help Me to Watch and Pray*

A Nazarene Mother Teresa in Boston: Esther Sanger

The simple handwritten sign tacked onto the telephone pole read, "If you need to talk to someone, call this number." Not many of us would dare to give out our phone number like that. Esther Sanger dared because she had come from a troubled past, knew the depths of loneliness, and had a friend who listened to her.

Esther came to Eastern Nazarene College as Midge Hicks— "Midge" because of her height of only 4'10". The dean of women, Esther Williamson, noticed her as someone who needed extra love. "Lady Willy," the affectionate name given her by students, took her under her wing and became the loving substitute mother she needed.

Esther was always faithful in church services. But doubts arose. In 1977 she began to seriously question her own faith. Was she truly Christian, or had she simply adopted the lifestyle of people she admired? To add to her dilemma, a severe case of food poisoning caused a prolonged stay in hospitals. Then a caring person sternly told her that she could either continue to turn inward and die or turn outward and live. She chose to live. "I peeled away the layers in my life, like peeling an onion," she said. "It was a frightening experience as I encountered emotions and attitudes of which I had not been aware." This soul-searching motivated by the Holy Spirit brought her to a renewed relation with Christ, and she found the identity of a relationship with God that brought peace to her soul and direction to her life. Esther now knew that the remainder of her life must be spent in helping others. That was when she posted the sign on the telephone pole.

People with great needs started to call. Esther not only listened but also found ways to help. At first she delivered groceries in her van. Then she realized she needed a central location. No one else in Quincy, Massachusetts, saw the need to help the hungry and homeless. Business and political ears were deaf to her pleas. So she decided to raise their awareness level. She parked an old motor home in front of City Hall and began serving food to the homeless. Any time city leaders looked out the office window, they saw the street full of homeless people being fed by a short woman who possessed a heart of love and a will of steel. It did not take long for city leaders to take steps to begin solving the problem.

While continuing this ministry of helps, Esther went back to Eastern Nazarene College for a degree in social work. With new insight and sensing God leading, she opened a central location to coordinate the work. With only $26 capital, she used her own home for that center, dubbing it the Quincy Crisis Center. Here the homeless, the hungry, the abused women and children, the frightened AIDS victims, the elderly—anyone desperate for help—could find someone who cared and offered a helping hand.

Next, Esther saw a need for single mothers and their little children, not only to shelter them, but also to teach the young mothers how to care for their children and how to stay off the streets. This dream became the Mary-Martha Learning Center, which now has its own place in nearby Hingham. Here she met with opposition from civic officials and neighbors who didn't want "those people" in their neighborhood. Again she chose to educate her opposition. She invited her neighbors in for coffee and talk and eventually won them over.

The Christian humanitarian concern also awakened a need for further training. Once more she turned to Eastern Nazarene College for a master's degree in family counseling. Feeling the further call of God, she began studying with a view to ordination as a minister whose parish was the world of the streets. She found a helpful base of relation and ministry as assistant pastor of Dorchester Second Church, a historic inner-city church that is now a Church of the Nazarene. This position gave her the opportunity to preach in churches of all denominations in the area of the South Shore. Her work became so well known in the communities of South Boston that a newspaper, *The Patriot Ledger,* called her the Mother Teresa of the South Shore.

Esther Sanger was ordained an elder in the Church of the Nazarene at the New England District Assembly in 1994. Many clergy members, including Nazarenes and those of other denominations, rejoiced with her. A little over a year later, in August, she died after a long struggle with cancer.

As the hospital chaplain, I spent many hours with her in her last illness. Sharing the Lord's Supper became times of blessing for us. Esther never complained—her concerns were for her children and her work.

The year following her death, the Esther R. Sanger Center for Compassion became the name for the vital ministries she started. Its two branches, the Mary-Martha Learning Center and the Quincy Crisis Center, continue to lengthen her life's shadow of service to desperate people. The ministry that began with $26 now has a yearly budget of nearly a million dollars.

No one who knew Esther when she first came to Eastern Nazarene College could have predicted these achievements. All her well-deserved honors and citations were as nothing to her in comparison to the "well done, good and faithful servant" commendation she has received from her Lord.

—*Ann Cubie Rearick*

A 20th-Century Study in Hebrews: Grayson and Zelma Tinker

Most of the stories in this book read like modern-day examples of the 11th chapter of Hebrews. This story is no exception. While a seminary student, I went to the Argentine section of Kansas City, Kansas, to plant a new church. We had only one interested Nazarene family in the area.

Soon the new church reached a middle-age couple named Grayson and Zelma Tinker. Neither could be considered potential leaders, but following the Lord, they became valiant in spiritual warfare. Zelma was a fine teacher of children but shy around adults. A sermon on witnessing gave her the courage to invite to church and dinner a couple they met at a Parent-Teacher Association meeting. Within a period of one year, that couple influenced another 36 people to come with them to church. This couple, the Scharnhorsts, have a son who is a Nazarene pastor and district Nazarene Youth International president. Imagine Zelma's surprise and joy to see her witness multiplied by God.

Grayson Tinker was shy and retiring, too, but as an employee of the Kansas City Power and Light Company, he had access to a record of new electric connections in the area around the church. Soon all those new people began to receive cards of invitation to the new Nazarene church.

After hearing Jarrette E. Aycock, "the district superintendent from skid row," testify about the man on the street in Los Angeles who invited him into the mission, Grayson decided he should do that. So he went often to the Kansas City Rescue Mission established by Aycock, stood outside on the sidewalk, and greeted everyone who went by, saying, "Why don't you come in? You might hear something that will do you good." That simple but faithful ministry influenced many to give their hearts to God.

Grayson had been raised in a sister Holiness church but wandered away because he felt no one was interested in young people. He decided that something should be done. Though he was not a carpenter, he found a sturdy building that could be turned into a gymnasium. He worked long and hard six days a week pulling nails from the old lumber so others could use it to build. He was preparing an "ark" for the saving of youth.

Then a freshman seminary student by the name of Ron Benefiel, now president of Nazarene Theological Seminary, was recruited to lead this youth ministry. The ministry also helped Grayson save his own family. Two of their sons became Nazarene pastors.

After Grayson's faithful wife, Zelma, died, he moved into a retirement center, where he continued being the same Spirit-empowered witness for Christ. He soon called his pastor to arrange for weekly gospel services at his new high-rise home. He spent his last days and strength visiting and inviting residents to the vesper services, always leaving them with prayer and an encouraging personal word.

In July 1996, the congregation, now known as Metropolitan Church of the Nazarene, celebrated its 50th anniversary. They now have a beautiful sanctuary, gymnasium, and parsonage. Across the years, six young people from this church have answered God's call to preach.

What a memory feast we enjoyed when five former pastors were honored on that golden anniversary day. But in that hour, my heart was especially warmed by the memory of so many dedicated laypersons who faithfully gave their time, money, prayer, and loyalty to advance God's cause through that local church. But I especially thanked God for Grayson and Zelma Tinker, who represent so many ordinary people who do extraordinary things for God. I take delight to think of them as standing in the middle of that grand biblical passage:

> *Wherefore, seeing we also are compassed about with so great a cloud of witnesses, let us lay aside every weight, and the sin which doth so easily beset us, and let us run with patience the race that is set before us* (Heb. 12:1, KJV).

—*George Rice*

The Treasurer Known as "Mr. Integrity": John Stockton

The business affairs of the church must always be above reproach. There is no substitute for complete honesty and accuracy in the accounting procedures. Paul wrote to the Corinthians, "Now it is required that those who have been given a trust must prove faithful" (1 Cor. 4:2). Paul repeated the same advice to the Romans when he wrote, "Be careful to do what is right in the sight of everybody" (Rom. 12:17).

John Stockton served as general treasurer of the Church of the Nazarene from 1945 to his retirement in 1970. He was the first to serve our denomination in this capacity full time. Before him, M. Lunn, in addition to managing Nazarene Publishing House, had filled that post for many years.

The years during which Stockton served in this office were a time of significant growth for the denomination. He will be remembered for establishing accounting practices and the management of church funds that moved the church into the demanding expectations of the modern business environment. The record shows that the General Budget of the church skyrocketed from $950,000 in 1945 to $6,750,000 by 1970.

From whence came his impeccable character and competent skills? Stockton was born in Chico, Texas, in 1899. He attended Bethany-Peniel College and began his banking career as a teller in the Farmers State Bank in Bethany. He soon moved to a larger bank in nearby Oklahoma City, and in 1938 he became manager of the Production Credit Corporation of Enid, Oklahoma, until 1941. In that position he managed loans made to farmers and ranchers in the surrounding counties. He managed over $4 million in loans, a large sum in those days, with all loans repaid on time.

In 1941 he returned to Bethany as business manager for the college. His love for Christ and for the church was the motivating factor in leaving a highly paid position and a bright future in government finance to take on the burdens of keeping a small college afloat financially.

One of his achievements as general treasurer has largely been overlooked. When G. B. Williamson was elected general superintendent, there existed a discrepancy in the rules of taxable income for pastors living in church-owned parsonages and those who owned their own homes. Dr. Stockton put together a team of legal advisers and provided the documentation that enabled the church to put together a test case, with Dr. Williamson as the petitioner, to go before the Federal Tax Court. The final ruling, stating that ministers who receive a housing allowance from a religious institution do not pay income tax on that allowance, has been a big boost for all ministers, not only of the Church of the Nazarene, but of all denominations.

In addition to his business acumen, John Stockton was an

interesting human being. I remember times when my family (the G. B. Williamsons) and the Stocktons would go out together. It was fun to listen to Dr. John order dessert. He would always ask the server to list all of the choices—sometimes he or she had to go over the list a second time—but he always ended up ordering vanilla ice cream. One time he was asked why he wanted to hear the selections, knowing he would order vanilla ice cream. He answered, "I always think there might be something that will sound better, but there never is."

One of my favorite memories of him was when we lived near the Stocktons in Kansas City. As a child, I had the usual curiosity-seeking wanderlust that gets many boys in trouble. There was a nearby streetcar line located on the other side of a busy street. It strongly engaged my curiosity but was out of bounds. The Stocktons lived where they could monitor my wanderings, so when I got too close to the forbidden boundary, there was either John or Ruth to send me home. Their kindliness left a lasting impression on me and maybe even saved my life.

A couple of verses from John Stockton's poem published in 1964, "Investments Here and Hereafter," explain the purpose of his life.

> *We're not working here for praise,*
> *   And we're not working here for glory,*
> *We're not worried greatly*
> *   Lest the world won't hear our story.*
>
> *But there's one thing we have wanted,*
> *   As down through life we've trod;*
> *That's to have the smile of Jesus*
> *   And the blessings of our God.*

—John Williamson

A Southern Gentleman Blesses His Church with Song: Hobson Byars

A great church is not always large, nor is a large church always great. A great church is one that honors Jesus Christ, lives a standard of holy living, ministers to its constituency, and reaches its arms around the world. Such a church must have outstanding laypersons who are faithful in all the life of the church.

Nashville First Church of the Nazarene has been blessed by many spiritually strong laypersons who fulfilled the Lord's command to be holy. Such people have supported and encouraged many strong pastors across the years.

Count among that number a true Southern gentleman named Hobson Byars. The list of his accomplishments as a layperson includes every office a layperson can hold. His service includes 65 years of devoted membership in a spirit that is winning as well as devoted. God gave him a golden voice with which to sing, and he has used it for the glory of God and the edification of the Church.

Hobson Byars was born in Millport, Alabama, in November 1906. His father was a schoolteacher and a Free-Will Baptist minister. Hobson came to Nashville to attend Vanderbilt University, but instead he enrolled and graduated from Trevecca Nazarene College in 1927. While there, he participated in many musical and sports activities. After graduation, he entered business and rose to be a manager for a large wholesale company.

In 1934 he married Gladys Damron, and they began attending Nashville First Church. He soon became a member and has been there ever since. He has served as Sunday School superintendent, president of the King's Men Missionary Chapter, and choir member, leading the singing when John T. Benson was away. He also brought people to church in his car, helped paint and repair the homes of the elderly, and was honoree at the church's Thanksgiving banquet one year.

Back during World War II, he served in the air force and was a handsome man in uniform. He was a striking figure when he sang "White Cliffs of Dover" or "I'll Be Home for Christmas." After the war, he returned to manage a nursing home and later became personnel director for two Nashville hospitals. His godly life and low-key personality stood him in good stead, and he was greatly appreciated by all who knew him.

In 1984 Hobson was named *Nazarene Weekly*'s honoree of the year. Written tributes from all over the country were published. Many spoke of the impact of his godly example, his gentle, gracious spirit, his unfailing kindness to everyone, and especially his God-given singing voice that has blessed thousands over the years.

Some of those written tributes noted that his Christian life is a model of commitment and faithfulness, and both his spirit and talent are channels through which blessings flow to all who know him. One person mentioned that he furnished transportation to and from church for her mother, little brother, and two small sisters during the depression years. Another noted that his music was spiritually encouraging and medically therapeutic when her mother was troubled in spirit and soul, that the Holy Spirit used his music to minister in unforgettable ways.

Over the years many were recipients of the use of his automobile to assist them when they were in need of help: the aged, the physically handicapped, and those who had no vehicle. One former pastor recalls that when he was a young pastor in Nashville in September 1936 for the district assembly, Hobson gave him a grand tour of the city in his car and was a gracious host. In this case, the grand tour was for me—a future pastor of Nashville First Church.

—*William M. Greathouse*

The Natives Called Her "Runner in the Gospel": Fairy Chism

In Swaziland when new missionaries arrive, the natives begin immediately to search for a name for them, watching mannerisms, dispositions, personalities, and priorities for clues. Soon after Fairy Chism arrived on the field, the Swazi Christians began to talk among themselves about how she ran everywhere she went. So before long, they decided their new missionary's Swazi name was Majubane—"a runner."

Toward the end of her third year at the Schmelzenbach station, after her dear friend and fellow missionary Louise Robinson was furloughed, the burden of the mission became overwhelming. She taught all day, oversaw the farming, pastored the local church, supervised eight outstations, served as mother to 75 girls at the school, and supervised the building of a new housing for the girls. These heavy responsibilities weighed upon her until she responded in a way that became a hallmark of her ministry—to wake at about four o'clock every morning to pray.

One morning as she prayed, God came marvelously, promising strength and wisdom for every need. From that day on, she reported that things seemed to run themselves.

Then one day the Swazis changed her name to "Majubane Wevangeli, "runner in the gospel," a name inscribed on her grave marker.

The little blue-eyed, curly-haired girl who grew up to be a pastor-missionary-evangelist was born in Arkansas in January 1899 to parents of hardy pioneer stock. Her mother, a godly woman of prayer, taught Fairy to pray as soon as she could put words together. At age 13, Fairy started a lifelong habit of reading the Bible through each year.

She was genuinely converted when in her teens during a revival in a Methodist church at Weiser, Idaho, and became an active leader in the youth group in the Moscow, Idaho, Methodist Church. Then a Nazarene evangelist came to Moscow and preached holiness in a home mission campaign. The Lord made it clear to the Chism family that this was to be their new church home. Fairy resigned the presidency of the Epworth League, though she loved her church and pastor, and joined the Church of the Nazarene in July 1918.

In September of that year, she enrolled at Northwest Nazarene College in Nampa, Idaho. It was there that her lifelong habit of prayer was established. When her mother complained that she was wearing out the toes of her shoes praying, her father, who was not a Christian at the time, said: "Now, Mother, you just let her alone. I'll buy her all the shoes she can pray through."

Fairy became a favorite speaker in the Boise Valley. In her senior year, her pastor, J. T. Little, insisted that she receive a preacher's license. When at her graduation there were no funds for new missionaries to be sent overseas, Fairy pastored three years at Halfway, Oregon, then two years at Baker, Oregon, before being assigned to Swaziland, where her friend Louise was already serving.

Fairy's lifelong habit of early-morning prayer resulted in a small "prayer hut" being erected behind her home. This became a standard part of her living quarters arrangement. It also caught on in other places. I even discovered a prayer hut on the grounds of the Papua New Guinea Bible college. When she finally came home to the United States, her friends in Lancaster, California, built her a home, and to complete it, they put a small concrete hut out back.

After 20 years in Swaziland, Fairy Chism felt that her time there was definitely through. Thus, in 1948 she returned home and spent another 20 years preaching as an evangelist in the United States and Canada with all the ardor and abandon that characterized her preaching to the Swazis.

Louise Robinson Chapman told about Fairy's first sermon in Swaziland. She had missed several meals, and Louise found her in her hut anguishing over her difficulty in learning the Zulu language. Fairy told her in tears, "I'm tired of doing nothing, saying nothing. God gave people the gift of language at Pentecost, and I'm determined to have the gift of Zulu before I leave this hut." Louise was able to convince her that she must study the language and the people until God helped her learn it.

Louise said, "On Fairy's first attempt to preach in Zulu, she used the text, 'The day of the Lord so cometh as a thief in the night' (1 Thess. 5:2). But the word for 'coming down' is very much like the one for 'coughing,' and the word for 'thief' is very similar to the one for 'wild beast.' Fairy confused these words and in her sermon repeated over and over 'The day of the Lord is coughing like a wild beast in the night.' A coughing wild beast in the night is a dreadful picture to a Swazi child. The sight of those little Africans listening to their missionary telling them of what is coming is with me yet" (*Africa, O Africa*, 10).

—*Fairy Hawthorne*

Devotion Produces Wise Investments:
Sam Snowbarger

Sam Snowbarger practiced dedicated stewardship like many other pioneers of the Church of the Nazarene. Under God's blessing, he owned two 160-acre farms—one was the homestead and the other an adjoining farm he had been able to purchase. He and his wife joined the Pleasant Hill Church of the Nazarene near Sylvia, Kansas, and became faithful members.

Then came the 1920s. Three great needs arose in institutions dear to Sam. The Kansas State Holiness Association camp meeting faced financial trouble. Word came that the Nazarene Publishing House might go broke. At the same time, Bresee College, located in Hutchinson, Kansas, was desperately in need of funds to stay in business. Sam took all this to heart and then to prayer. In response to what he believed to be God's will, he gave far beyond his cash reserves.

While financial advisers say you should never use borrowed money for investment, Sam went beyond such prudence because he was interested in eternal investments. First he mortgaged the 160-acre farm adjacent to the homestead and then the homestead. Along with many others, his giving helped the camp meeting survive, the publishing house continue to print Holiness literature, and Bresee College stay open to train young people for a life of service.

Then there came eight terrible years of drought and depression. The 1929 crash and the Great Depression followed. Crops failed, mortgages were foreclosed, and the nation was in bankruptcy. The long years of drought caused one Kansas farmer to sing mournfully, "O Kansas land, dry Kansas land, / As on thy burning sands I stand, / I look away across the plains / And wonder why it never rains, / And when I turn and view my corn, / I almost wish I'd ne'er been born."

In such troubled times, the Federal Land Bank began foreclosing on mortgages. Most families were wiped out financially. Sam first lost the adjoining farm; then the loan on the homestead came due. When the administrator came to the Snowbarger home, he said, "Mr. Snowbarger, there is every reason for me to foreclose on this mortgage. But I want to tell you as I moved through this community, several people told me, 'Whatever you do to me, don't foreclose on Sam Snowbarger.'" As a result, the time was extended, and Sam was eventually able to pay off the loan. His neighbors knew that he had risked everything for worthy causes that really mattered.

God honored Snowbarger with amazing results. All nine of his children graduated from Nazarene colleges, and two earned advanced degrees. All became faithful supporters of Nazarene churches. Most of his grandchildren and great-grandchildren take their church relations seriously. One of his grandchildren said, "I can remember him as a joyful Christian, testifying, starting a song in prayer meeting. He enjoyed a good joke and always had a twinkle in his eye."

Though he may have been considered a foolish investor by worldly standards, he considered himself a faithful steward expected to use God's resources in Kingdom interests. He said and believed, "All I have is the Lord's, and He has loaned me the use of the land." To him, that meant only heavenly gains are permanent. Therefore, he believed it wise to take what you cannot keep and invest it where you cannot lose it. In fact, his stewardship took his possessions out of the hands of bankers and beyond the impact of droughts, depressions, moths, rust, or thieves. He transferred his holdings to an account administered by the Heavenly Investor, who deals in eternal values.

Imagine yourself drinking in spiritual inspiration at a camp meeting or standing on the campus of a thriving Nazarene university or watching the mail trucks load at Nazarene Publishing House. All this is possible because of the sacrifices of persons like Sam Snowbarger. Then realize Sam and many others like him deserve part of the reward for every success these ministries are now having.

Sam Snowbarger taught everyone who knew him to

Trust in the Lord with all your heart
and lean not on your own understanding,
in all your ways acknowledge him,
and he will make your paths straight.

—Prov. 3:5-6

—*Willis E. Snowbarger*

They Kept the Doors Open So I Could Walk In: Joe and Shirley Mormino

The Fox Lake church had fallen on bad times. Job transfers, divisions, misunderstandings, and stubborn selfishness had taken a terrible toll on attendance. No one except the Morminos expected the church to survive.

Joe and Shirley Mormino were the only two present on Sunday, May 3, 1978, when I visited for the first time. The situation was embarrassing for them and for me, but they were determined to keep the doors open, and I'm glad they did.

When my two stepchildren and I arrived at the Fox Lake, Illinois, Church of the Nazarene at 10:30 that Sunday morning, the Morminos extended a warm greeting to the new threesome. They said, "We're sorry about the low attendance, but we've had problems. All of our people are gone, we have no pastor, but we felt it was important to keep the doors open."

I replied, "We've decided to come to church today, and the size of the crowd is not important." The five who met that day believed God was with them.

"Do you play the piano?" Joe asked.

"Yes," I answered.

"Thank the Lord—you're an answer to prayer."

The Lord kept His word: "Where two or three of you are gathered together in my name, there am I in the midst of you." As our attendance grew, we discovered that when 20 were counted, there were really 21, and when the count was 39, it was really 40.

Joe and Shirley were not really noticeable people. But his job as a truck driver gave him plenty of time to pray. It was obvious that they were a very devoted couple. He always wore a suit on Sunday. They were both courteous at all times. This couple continued their faithfulness, opening the doors twice on Sunday and also on Wednesday for prayer meeting. They made calls to follow up on every visitor. They scheduled dinners and furnished the food. Despite the discouragement, they continued to pray for a pastor.

Then in July, just two months later, they had a pastor who suggested, "Let's have a Vacation Bible School in August." And they did, averaging 30 in attendance despite the shortage of time, teachers, materials, and experience.

Joe and Shirley believed in the power of prayer. Shirley and the new pastor's wife started a weekly time of prayer and Bible study for the ladies. Their constant prayer was that the church would grow, and it did. The spirit of unity that prevailed resulted in a similar event that happened in the second chapter of Acts: "The Lord added to their number daily those who were being saved" (v. 47). On Christmas Sunday 1979, just a year after Joe and Shirley stood by themselves in the church foyer, 45 attended the morning worship service.

Though it was getting late in their lives, Joe accepted a call of God to the ministry. He continued to drive his truck as he took the correspondence course and finished it while still being faithful to his church. He pastored churches in Illinois and Indiana and then in May 2000, just 22 years after the Fox Lake church had been at its lowest point, he went home to be with the Lord.

By human standards, this record might not be considered a great success. But when I think of their warm welcome that helped to restore my relationship with the Lord, I am reminded that God's final measure of success will be the measure of our faithfulness to Him. It is the Joe and Shirley Morminos and their faithfulness that God will honor on the final day. They were faithful to their calling—to plant and water. And, like He promised, "God gave the increase" (1 Cor. 3:6, KJV).

—*Gayle Sears*

⊷ ⚔ ⊶

The Lady Said, "I Can Do," with God's Help: Ruth Carter

Consider these obstacles to a personal faith and maintaining a Christian home: A frontier neighborhood favoring saloons, dance halls, and other detrimental entertainment. Add an unsaved and antagonistic husband. Mix in household duties that included four children, cooking for hired hands, helping with farm-work, canning foods, sewing for the family, and a lack of electricity. Then consider a limited education and a home mission church made up of women like herself who were spiritual widows with husbands unsaved or too busy for church. Then go to the Lord in prayer about the problem.

This faithful woman had prayed, *O Lord, save my children—You can't let the devil get my children.* The Lord's answer was, "Are you willing to do for other people's children what you will do for your own children? You see, I'm interested in them too."

But wait a minute, Lord. I don't have the education, and You see how much work I have to do already, with no help from my husband.

The Heavenly Father persisted: "But I want to save the others too, and you won't be able to do it just for your own—you will need the others too."

When Ruth Carter finally said yes to God's call to teach, she found her own lifelong philosophy of service: "You *can do* with God's help."

With a newfound dedication and zeal, she went to the other mothers of the little church. She told them, "It's not enough to tell the children where they can't go and what they can't do—we must give them something positive that they can do and provide places where they can go."

They found the solution worked. They provided Bible studies, parties, and dinners almost every Sunday. Then there were programs. Every special day had a program, and every program involved all the young people. No one was left out. Everyone had a "part" to get the message across and to learn to do God's work by doing.

Soon there came the district youth camps. Mrs. Carter was always a chaperone. She would put the sideboards on the farm truck, load in the bedrolls and suitcases, have the kids climb in on top, and off they went. One year they had 32 youth there, the largest crowd of any church on the district.

One year at youth camp, Ruth Carter was burdened until she fasted. Day after day she fasted, over seven days, until every one of her children was either saved or sanctified or called to preach. Of the 30 who were there that year, 7 became preachers or missionaries.

Did all these victories solve the problem at home? Well, not yet. A seasonal evangelist came to the church. The family, all but the husband, went to church. The preacher was invited to stay in the Carter home. After some resistance, the husband finally relented, but when they came home from church, he had erected a sign in purple ink: "Preacher's Roost." There was tension, then a good laugh, and the husband and the evangelist became good friends.

Praying, teaching, and practicing hospitality, Mother followed Dad from one irrigation project to another, pioneering always in a new place, living in a house while it was being built, or living in an unfinished house because rationed building materials were not easy to come by during World War II. However, her unbelieving husband was finally won to the Lord before he died. Her former pastor, Jim Bond, wrote to her in 1985, "You have constructed with your life a monument that shall forever stand as a rebuke to easygoing, complacent, and lifeless Christianity."

Former pastor Jerald Johnson referred to her as "the best backyard evangelist I ever knew." She looked out her window one time and saw a family walking by who appeared to be from India. She ran down the steps and hailed them, "Are you from India?" "Yes," they said. "My son and his family were missionaries in central India, and I've come to love Indian people." She asked them in for tea, made friends, and invited them to church. She tutored them in English, using the Gospel of John as a textbook. Pastor Johnson was instrumental in leading them to the Lord.

Some time after becoming a widow, Mother married Joseph Penn, a missionary to Africa. She had become an educated woman following God's call in self-directed study. God proved His promise: "You *can do* with My help." And she did.

—*Norma Ernest and Marianne Carter Williams*

The Missionary Whom Miracles Followed: Everette D. Howard

In a small, two-room cabin located on the edge of a large cotton field near Burlison, Tennessee, Everette D. Howard was born July 15, 1906. His mother died when he was four, and his father, Rev. C. J. Howard, moved to College Mound, Missouri, to attend a Holiness college. Other Nazarene leaders who attended that school included A. E. Sanner, G. B. Williamson, and D. I. Vanderpool.

Later, Rev. C. J. Howard moved to Colorado, where he pastored at Yuma, Boulder, and Lamar. Everette enjoyed going in a buggy with his father to make his calls. Young Everette's musical ability consisted of three chords, which he used on an old, worn-out pump organ to play any song in the hymn book. The local church named him director of music and later assistant pastor.

From Lamar, Colorado, he hitchhiked to Pasadena, California, to go to college. His education was furthered when his father became pastor at Pittsburg, Kansas, home of Kansas State Teachers' College. His father asked Garnet Sherman, one of the young ladies in the church, to walk the two miles with Everette and help him arrange his classes. This was most providential and probably not without some forethought on the pastor's part.

Garnet was the daughter of Mr. and Mrs. I. C. Sherman, strong members of the Pittsburg church. I. C. Sherman was a longtime trustee of the church and Mrs. Sherman a loved Sunday School teacher who often had 75 in her class of young married couples. Garnet was the jewel that Everette needed. She was his most loyal booster, best friend, levelheaded adviser, as well as a devoted wife. When their wedding was announced at the time of their graduation from college, the church named him assistant pastor. Then one week before the wedding, Rev. C. J. Howard was in an accident and died as a result of his injuries. After the funeral, Everette's stepmother took his half-brother, Bill, and moved to Lamar, Colorado.

After their wedding, Everette finished the three months of that assembly year as pastor of the Pittsburg church and then was appointed pastor at Ottawa, Kansas. It was while pastoring in Ottawa that both Everette and Garnet believed they were called as missionaries to the Cape Verde Islands. So they went to present their case to J. G. Morrison, then general secretary of foreign missions. Each time they made the 65-mile trip from Ottawa to

Nazarene Headquarters in Kansas City, Dr. Morrison told them the church was scraping the bottom of the barrel and that no money was available to send new missionaries anywhere.

That's about the time their missionary miracles started. After being told the same story on several trips to Kansas City and Dr. Morrison becoming somewhat annoyed, Garnet wrapped a beautiful gift for him. When Dr. Morrison started his story about the barrel, they kindly interrupted and said, "Dr. Morrison, we have come today to give you a gift. It has helped us, and we think it will help you believe God will open doors for us to go to Cape Verde." The package contained a copy of the book titled *Achieving Faith*. He laughed and cried. At the same time, his secretary came in with a telegram from the New York and New England districts that read, "We have united to open work on the Cape Verde Islands. We will pay the way to the field and support a couple for two years, providing you know anyone who is called to this field." Everette and Garnet went home to pack and were soon on their way to Cape Verde.

Then there was the water miracle on Fogo Island. It is considered to have one of the largest active volcanos in the world and one of the most perfectly formed. It rises suddenly out of the Atlantic Ocean 300 miles west of the African coast. The top of the cone may be seen for miles. It looks as if some Niagara of molten rock had poured down the sides of the mountain, then crystallized into fantastic shapes.

But there was no water on the island. When Everette visited the people there, his ration of water for one day was one glass. That was to wash, shave, brush his teeth, and drink with. Added to the normal drought, there had been no rain for five years. People and animals were dying. Pastors Ilidio Silvia and Luciano Barros had led their people in deep devotion and faith. One day Pastor Barros challenged the people to pray for rain. They anchored their faith on Isa. 41:17-18. The next morning, just at dawn as the sun was rising out of the vast Atlantic Ocean down below, something happened. Pouring out of the side of that volcanic mountain of solid rock was a fountain of water—pure, fresh water. And it has continued to flow through the years.

Then there was the leper along the wayside. Everette and

Pastor de Silva were walking along a black sandy beach when they came across a half-starved skeleton of a young man who had tried to cover himself with the black sand for warmth at night. They prayed. He prayed. The Lord forgave him his sins. Then the Lord healed him—completely. Four days later, the young man carried Everette's accordion on his head to another village.

Then there was the Maude Chapman Memorial Church miracle. Everette had been led by the Lord to seek a building site. The government officials put every possible obstacle in his way. But Everette persisted. Several years of finagling and conniving on the part of the officials and they were still stymied. It was a choice property. When erected, the cross on the steeple would tower over every other building in Praia, the capital city. Time after time, the lots would go up for sale, and there was always a priest there to outbid the Nazarenes. Then they would default and have another sale. On the day of the sale, Everette was there and bought the location just before the priest rushed up shouting, "You can't do this!" But it had already been done.

On one New Year's Eve, the Howards were home on furlough in Pittsburg, Kansas. We had scheduled him to show some more of his pictures from 9 until 10. There came an ice storm. Trees were uprooted, electric power lines downed, and the city in darkness. We had candles in the church to carry on the service. Just at 9 P.M., the lights came on in the church. Everette's last picture was on the screen when the lights went off again, at 10 P.M.

Garnet's health worsened over the years. Before she died, she told Everette that when she did pass away, he was to marry Lydia Wilke, a dear friend and fellow missionary. He said, "No, I'll never do that!" But she said, "Everette, you like honey on your toast in the morning, and I'm afraid you'll go to church some morning with honey on your tie!" After Garnet's death, Lydia and Everette, living at Casa Robles—the missionary retirement home in California—were on their way to church. Lydia remarked, "Everette, Garnet told me before she died what she told you, and I just want to tell you, there's honey on your tie this morning!" They married soon after.

—*L. Wayne Sears*